THE SOUTHERN POETRY ANTHOLOGY

VOLUME VIII

TEXAS

Printed in the United States of America

FIRST EDITION, 2018

Cover design by Chad M. Pelton
Cover photo by Paul Ruffin

A brief word about the below information: The Library of Congress directed us to use the CIP data from the first volume of the anthology, even though we have distinct data for other volumes. The correct publication information is listed below, before this data:

Title: The Southern Poetry Anthology, VIII: Texas
Editors: William Wright, and Paul Ruffin
ISBN: 978-1-68003-063-1 (Paper)
ISBN: 978-1-68003-064-8 (ebook)

Library of Congress Cataloging-in-Publication Data

The Southern poetry anthology : South Carolina / [compiled] by Stephen Gardner and
William Wright — 1st ed.
p. cm.
ISBN: 978-1-68003-063-1 (pbk. : alk. paper)
1. American poetry—South Carolina. I. Gardner, Stephen. II. Wright, William, 1979-
PS558.S6S68 2007
811.008'09757—dc22
2007023711

THE SOUTHERN POETRY ANTHOLOGY

VOLUME VIII

TEXAS

William Wright, *Series Editor*

Paul Ruffin & William Wright, *Volume Editors*

PREVIOUS VOLUMES

William Wright, Series Editor

Volume I: South Carolina
Edited by Stephen Gardner and William Wright

ISBN-10: 193389606X
ISBN-13: 978-1933896069

Volume II: Mississippi
Edited by Stephen Gardner and William Wright

ISBN-10: 1933896248
ISBN-13: 978-1933896243

Volume III: Contemporary Appalachia
Edited by Jesse Graves, Paul Ruffin, and William Wright

ISBN-10: 1933896647
ISBN-13: 978-1933896649

Volume IV: Louisiana
Edited by Paul Ruffin and William Wright

ISBN-10: 1933896779
ISBN-13: 9781933896779

Volume V: Georgia
Edited by Paul Ruffin and William Wright

ISBN-10: 1933896939
ISBN-13: 9781933896939

Volume VI: Tennessee
Edited by Jesse Graves, Paul Ruffin, and William Wright

Volume VII: North Carolina
Edited by Jesse Graves, Paul Ruffin, and William Wright

ISBN-13: 978-1-937875-87-9
ISBN 10: 1937875873

This volume is dedicated with love to the memory of Paul Ruffin

CONTENTS

Series Editor's Note

This brief beginning belies a volume with a long, complex history.

This eighth volume of *The Southern Poetry Anthology* is dedicated to Paul Ruffin, who directed Texas Review Press for almost forty years and who passed away in 2016. To say he worked hard for writers, and in particular Texas writers, is an almost absurd understatement. The latter part of his writing life was spent energizing other writers as much as, and probably more, than his own literary life.

The consequence of such choices unfortunately diluted the reputation of his entire *ouevre*, particularly his poems and fiction, a situation that I and others who knew his giftedness hope to remedy.

But let me speak of the volume you're holding, a long overdue collection of very special writers. Paul's death, mixed with a rather large dose of personal issues, protracted the book's construction from one year into three. Nonetheless, I hope the poems herein make the contributors and the readers proud and partially atone for the long time they have had to wait for them.

I thank Kim Davis, Claude Wooley, Larry D. Thomas, Jeffrey Alfier, Naomi Shihab Nye, Nick Lantz, and Dave Parsons for their encouragement, good cheer, and help in locating certain Texan poets. Kim Davis, who worked as interim director of Texas Review Press, has been a paragon of kindness, good humor, and optimism. Last and most certainly not least, I thank my wife Michelle, whose spirit inspires me every day. Doubtless I am forgetting to thank many, as this book, the result of a dynamic collaborative spirit running through the poets in this great state, has humbled me.

I am grateful for all contributors' long-standing patience and for trusting me with their poems. I thank this book's readers and know the poems herein will serve as inspiration for many. And, finally, I thank Paul Ruffin again for believing in my ability to create—and to continue—this vast and rewarding series.

William Wright
Marietta, GA

Carolyn Adams

Live from the Moon

The attic fan sucks
another humid Houston summer
into the house.
But you can't see that
in the photo.
You can't see
the chicken wire fences,
the half-mowed yards,
the kids coming in late
for supper.
The little three by five
only records
a lit blue screen,
captioned with
"LIVE FROM MOON,"
and a fat doll, mid-hop
in a bulbous white suit,
planting a toothpick flag
on a desolate landscape.
You can't hear
the incredulous announcer
narrating the doll's clumsy moves
as if they're part
of a dramatic play,
not the light opera they appear.
You can't see
a kid slamming a screen door,
running outside
to stare at the naked moon,
searching for spacemen
crawling
its dirty white face.

Subtraction

It's a simple picture.
A woman in a flowered dress
pushes the family mower
through the tall grass
between the ditch
and the fence line.

It's early morning,
shadows are long
on the ground behind her.
Wind billows her skirt,
pushes her hair
from her upturned face,
and you can see she isn't pretty.
But there's a homeliness
you'd feel comfortable with.
Like a warm supper,
a strong hand, fresh sheets
on a backyard line.

She strains at the task,
pushing the machine
through the tangled weeds,
in an imagined arithmetic.
Subtracting today
from tomorrow,
tomorrow from yesterday,
right now
from never.

Leslie Marie Aguilar

Panhandle

For Kurt

In the panhandle, thrushes nest
by bell towers that ring out across

acres of thistle—a landscape of exile.
Here exile is rain. Rain is punishment,

& creeks fill with layers of rust.
In the panhandle, snow is cotton-

covered highways & barbed-wire
posts guarding aluminum shacks.

In the panhandle, drought is justice
for planting cotton on barren plains,

where everyone leans into the wind
instead of against it as storms roll in.

In the panhandle, clouds are steeples
for a church of rain no one believes in,

where dust is a communion of palms
raised against the sky like open fists.

Water Mexican

Barreling through the air like a bare-knuckled fist,
I am raw hide & pink panties clinging to the edge
of my narrow hips as I leap into a turquoise tiled
swimming pool. I am a child, & I have not learned
how to swim yet, have not learned to thrash my limbs
violently beneath the surface to keep my head afloat.
I must have known then, the moment before I flopped
belly first into the pool, that I would float to the surface.

Years later, when my white friend asks if I can swim,
I will lower my head toward the creek bed beneath
the cypress bridge where we are standing & say, *no,*
there are snakes in this water. Gesturing with her index
finger, she will point at the water moccasins gliding
beneath the water & say, *but those Mexicans can swim.*
We will laugh at the slip of her tongue, not knowing
then water moccasins are venomous snakes that patrol
waters of Southern states. When the bridge collapses,
years later, I will have learned how to tread water,
& my friend will have learned how to swim faster.

Sapo Sister

Are you the one who carries the moon?
I am the sunscald along the bottom
of your backyard canyon, blistering
anise & amethyst beneath your feet.

I am sunscald along the bottom-bed
of a scorched lake where you grow
anise & gather amethyst birthstones
for waterless children without names.

The lake where you wait, patiently,
is a puddle of rain without remedies.
Without water, the barren names are
sung as faint bone dry bolo ballads.

Can this puddle be a remedy without rain?
You thread peppermint & periwinkle
into bolo ties like shoestring necklaces
bound with silver tumbled turquoise.

You thread peppermint & periwinkle
talismans beneath a lunar halo light.
Bound in silver anklets & turquoise,
you wait for the final transmutation.

Beneath the weight of this lunar halo,
in your blistering backyard canyon,
you are transformed as by design.
You are the one who carries the moon.

Lahab Assef Al-Jundi

Ghosts

Our house is not old enough
to have ghosts haunting
or tinkering at night.
The only spirits we encounter here
are those of old encinos
and cedars that gave us room to root
in the white rock of the hill country.
They come whispering to old friends
now with trimmed St. Augustine at their feet.

Someday, long after we are gone, another man,
another woman,
will be living here
under this great sloped canopy.
Their eyes will meet the gaze
of curious midnight moons
through wakeful high windows.

Even then,
my big brown recliner will wait
facing the white rocks of the fireplace.
It will creak
under the weight
of my invisible body.

They will hear it.
Stop. Wonder.

Another sound. A long swish
as if
someone is blowing over the edge
of a hot cup of tea.

Ghosts
of an old encinos
returning.

Lou Amyx

Old Man

You buried three wives.
Three children.
The three-legged chow that wandered into the yard,
          stinking, his skin being eaten by mange.
Dropped him with a .38 pistol shot
          from the top of the driveway.
The clean hit left a small bloodless hole.
          I helped you drag the body.

It was hot when you decided the grave was deep enough.

I washed the shovels while you made sandwiches.
We drank beer from frozen glasses.
You told the story of the lightning and the greenbroke mare,
          tomato dripping onto your plate.

Wendy Barker

Thunder

To Descartes, one cloud falling
onto another. To the Greeks,
Zeus's shield shaking, a forerunner
of Hopkins' shook foil, that grandeur,
gathered and charged. For the native
tribes of the plains, Thunderbird's
wings beating. Such magnified
oscillations are beyond us, yet
the very air we breathe is grumbling,
a succession of compressions,
negative and positive ions colliding,
as someone in the next room
is about to explode.

Trash

"Trash," he said, as we walked the line
between our almost-country properties.
Again I pointed, trees and shrubs
whose names I didn't know, but "trash,"
he said again. Anything not oak.

That neighbor knew three kinds of trees:
live, pin, and Spanish oak. The rest should go.
And now I've lived here twenty years
I know how chainsaws take out everything
that isn't oak, not just the junipers

that choke the other plants nearby, but also
Texas buckeyes, magenta blooming in
the spring, redbuds, huisachillo, sweet acacia.
Mexican persimmon's bark blends velvet
grays and silky browns, its rounded leaves

bright yellow-green before the purple fruit
draws birds that nest on into June—
buntings and the wrens above the grasses,

gramas and the bluestems. November,
the seed heads in waves of burgundy, of red.
Our city council said they'd leave the trees
when clearing for the city hall. But like
that neighbor years ago, they meant
the oaks. Now they've called a meeting.
Oak wilt has hit the neighborhood, and

oaks are what we're left with. Too much
construction, trimming of the trees, their
wounds not treated. The virus travels
through the maze of connecting roots.
And once a tree's infected, it's trash.

Inheritance

After my father died, my mother talked of a tree
she had seen at the edge of a field in fall:
a great tree as if on fire, she said, and she wanted
the rest of her life to be like that, one blaze
before the leaves fell, before it all was gone.
Now in the entry near her front door hangs a print
of a winter tree, rounded, heavy, white with snow.

Late winter, you and I have walked this way so often.
I thought I knew what to expect, oaks dropping
their brittle leaves, pushed off by their own buds.
Juniper, scrub. Grasses bent, shadowed with mold.

There is never a way to describe the things that rise
before you. A flush of white straight ahead, a breath
lifting. We turn from the path we'd been following,
into the mud of an abandoned road, to face this scent
of blossom, these circling bees, this bursting:
an old pear, gone back to its wild, original rootstock,
blooming over its intricate branches, a perfect oval.

Curtis Bauer

If This Is What It Takes

The knife in your hand wants flesh–
its appetite for blood is sharp steel
leaning, weeping into the tomato's meat,
sugar beets, steaming rhubarb pie–and hunts
that juice etching your hands, pulsing
your neck and shifting your hips. You
slice, you bleed, you leak into pools bubbling
the countertop, over the scuffed linoleum
to the stainless steel sink and anoint the potato
peelings, onion skins and apple rinds.
Make your salad before rot sets in
and that side of you that turns my head
after we've parted on the street
to watch your steps escapes. You come to me
squeezing your bleeding as if it were a gift,
as if the more you bled the better you'd feel
offering your invitation to join the thin red
sliver seething and throbbing your hands
into mine. Beautiful bleeder, my hands
never held holy powers until they entangled yours.
A blade, I understand its language. Give me
the knife and press its edge here. Pull.

Alan Birkelbach

Ultimately

> *Linnaeus believed in the Grand Design. In his system there was no mechanism of change because God designed all organisms perfectly the first time.*
> –The Day The Universe Changed, *James Burke*

Having spent the last twenty minutes
trying to untangle the conical wire tomato cages
and realizing in a taxonomic, evolving kind of way
they are related to coat hangers,

I sit here now on a hot metal lounge chair on the patio
sipping a beer and realizing with no little pride
that I fought the many-spindly-legged beast
to a standstill.

It is at moments like this, sweaty and slightly inebriated,
my brain swerves towards phrases and metaphors.
Linnaeus, straight man that he was,
wouldn't have liked the word swerve.

Perhaps I would mention to him the taunting squirrels
who have not learned their place In this grand scheme.
Or the lizard who has learned to visit my front door to remind me if I don't
sweep the dead bugs he will take care of it.

That might not be enough to set Linnaeus spinning.
So I will mention that evidently God did not design
the wear and tear clause in my lease. Nor did the Almighty
have a finger on the depreciation of my car.

And I suspect it wasn't him who made me buy
the magic rotisserie-oven off late-night TV
that broke ten minutes after I got it out of the box.
Linnaeus–I am not done.

God is also probably not the mind behind
"new and improved stickers." Granted, He might be the one

who has helped me be content with the piles of laundry I accumulate—
the whole reverting to a natural state thing—but probably not.

Yet, Linnaeus, I still believe that everything has its place.
Currently, my butt belongs in this hot lawn chair.
And this beer belongs in my hand.
The tangled snarl of tomato cages belongs
on the other side of the yard.

There's an order here, a balance—
my own personal Versailles.
And even so, when the squirrels dig holes willy-nilly,
and the tomatoes die an untethered death,
there will still be more than enough blame to go around.

Suzette Bishop

Prairie Beekeeper

Parched, sweating,
long skirt dragging in dust,
checking on hives.

No need to talk,
brushing your hand
over the swarm,
unafraid,
gentle.

There's activity
and sleep,
mothers
and children,
males just for mating,
a livelihood,
a setting sun
burnishing low clouds,
a cooling wind
drying your dampened nape.

Bee Hex

Deranged
social arrangements,
chambers,
cells,
no one tells you anything useful
or that makes sense,
a manic uncommunicative hum,
an imploding colony.

Carry your heaviness
toward the sun
or wait in your chamber
until the prickling feeling
ends.

A whole parade,
amputated, bulging,
floating away,
no energy to reach
the cold fields,
a buzzing toward the sun.
Disappear

or turn away from the others,
choose your own hexagonal coffin,
your own honeycomb grave.

Roberto Bonazzi

Intermezzi

I

From the writing studio
I amble over backyard pavers,
up deck stairs into the house.

II

Returning between blue *intermezzi*
across a wilted green oasis, never
count steps or words.

III

Stopping to rearrange pot plants,
I wonder at suggestive clouds,
an unexpected cold wind.

IV

Far away, our brother died today.
Leaves turn yellow and red.
Crisp brown ones fall.

Solitary Grief

for Lawrence (1942–2014)

Appearing silently
in insomnia's notebook,
hidden in an old heavy chest.

Hearing Bach's violin solos,
the cat lets out a little yelp.

Twin's arrow opens old wounds.
Stages never inhabit predicted pattern,
yet mourners act according to script.

Solitude overcomes indulgence.
Empathy shorn of self-pity.

Unheard of declensions arise.

Withdrawals

Shallow sips of cognac with evening descending.

We do not learn our strengths until we are vulnerable.
Sadness our most intense feeling, although only aging knows.

Ego weeded out the gray hairs, later trimmed dark ones.
Humility never brought scissors to the mirror.

Withdrawing from clichés of wisdom,
settling dust settles nothing, playing
bagatelles on a loose tooth.

Bruce Bond

Gold Bee

Invention is the mother of invention,
and so the bee coated in gold, arrested

in flight, pays homage to the lens that sees it,
to the microscope of the new century

that made this gilt a necessary thing.
For gold loves an electron, carries it

along the bloodless vein of the wing,
thrilled in stillness, to make a sharper image.

What then are these electrons if not bee-
bound for the hungry flower of the eye.

A bee like that is everywhere you want
to be: everywhere the whir of wings

that halo the hidden violence of attraction.
If this is one more music of the spheres,

it goes unheard because we always hear it.
Like those first few months when we were tiny.

The eye too is a haloed thing, an angel
gilded in the light of foreign objects

that come and go, and the eye burns on.
Likewise the meadows that are the mother

of bees who give, in turn, birth to meadows
that pull at heaven and earth to be seen.

Their corruption is everywhere, as blooms
that pay the boatman to ferry their gold away.

Or so says the thrum of petals no one
hears, the blurred wings of ghost essentials

we coat in the flown colors of spring.
Can you blame us if we sweep the floor

of bees and sing to see them fly a little.
Those in mourning know what it is

to occupy a space of great stillness,
an ideal that's never perfect for good

reason. It's ideal. Sealed in honey
like the sad bells and cathedrals of Prague.

Or the pharaoh's coffin glazed in metal
for the journey. Gold dreams the long dream

of an underworld economy.
It would stabilize the terms of give

and take, the forces of impoverishment
and fortune that litter meadows in their season.

Nature envelops nature and calls it new
as death is new and violent and still and never

still enough. If you look hard there,
you can always see something moving.

It is your eye looking hard, moving in.
In as in the word *invention: in venire*,

an entering. Always a child inside us,
grown small, a steeple and the thread of day,

poorly remembered, that passes through.
Inside every memory there is another,

a place that waits with the patience of heaven.
Always a speck of dust, quick as music,

and made things that would make the maker.
They're in there, the powers of invention

that open something: the bee the blossom, the blossom
the eye, the eye the bee-gold eye of bee.

Ink

When, in the dark ages of the east,
the Mongols took the heart of the city
and poured in, room after room, to cut
a path through the bodies in their way,
they loaded up the illuminated books,
the many wildflowers of Islam hand-sewn,
penned, edged in gold, and made of them
a bridge across the Tigris, shaky at best,
to lead men from the spoils of their labor.
This is the story of the House of Wisdom,
how centuries gathered there to pool
the gems of medicine and metaphysics,
until the river took them, leaving us
the ache of knowing just enough to ache.
If history repeats, it does so without us.
It returns the way a criminal returns,
or a tongue to the space that was a tooth.
When the bodies of the philosophers
broke the surface, they floated here and there,
littering the shore, their wounds drained
into the current, to stain the glass
not red exactly, in spite of what you hear,
but rust, a fading scar of dirt and iron.
The greatness of a city is how it kneels
near the water, to beat its laundry there,
or flood the fields in their season, to carry
what: fennel, flax, cinnamon, a scholar.
Beyond the necessary, a river draws
the mourner toward something she cannot find—
it helps her nonetheless—or the believer
toward reconciliation with her god.
If we hear there rumors of water going
on without end, it is none the less loss
that speaks. What book would not be a bridge.
Or the grave of some sad misconception.
Somewhere still there is a volume that says
what the river of the dead cannot,
that once a library fell into the Tigris,
and these waters, that are a widow's friend,
ran black with ink, mile after mile.

The Invisible Hand

Our life has no end the way our visual field has no limits.
–Ludwig Wittgenstein

Light, we know, is an invisible thing.
The beam that falls through the theaters
of a childhood—we trust it's there

thanks only to the dust that floats inside it,
and the screen, of course, the stuff that takes
the dark of light and makes of it a story.

In this way light provides a language
for the dawn of things, ourselves, for instance,
how we travel through the first two years

into the luminous amnesia of who
we are, blind to the gods of days that made us.
A body might be replaced twelve,

thirteen times over, every cell hung
on the architecture of what goes missing,
the way the widow hangs on her son's arm,

on the strength inside his long black sleeve.
Today I listened to Ravel's *Concerto*
for the Left Hand, to its vague beginnings

in the bass violins, the rocking cradle
of the bow as if it were tuning up
for what's to come, for the slow emergence

of a subject, the polish of the brass,
the great wave that peaks and washes ashore
the hand, the A, the lowest of the keys.

It's the announcement of our soloist
whose body lies buried in the ghost
of sound. Do you think of him as well,

Paul Wittgenstein, the man who lost his arm
to a Russian bullet, how he woke
in a prison hospital to find it gone.

He could not see this yet as the birth
of all the left-hand scores he would commission,
Ravel's, for one. In truth, music's origins

are the casualties of every age.
Given time days wept a pool of light
over charcoal keys he sketched on a crate.

And as he taught his hand to play the parts
that were not there, the reach of it grew
desperate, quick, as if it were two hands,

worlds apart, one dead, another living,
each one abandoned by the other,
bound by that to the talk between them.

What is more intangible than the past
to come. Remember, him on stage, the tuck
of the sleeve that fluttered in its pins.

I have seen his performance in a movie,
his hand leaping like a bird on fire,
as if all he lost brought on an excess

of life. The madness and the suicides
of a tragic family—they can break you
down or open, or a little of both.

You can almost hear him as he turns
to his brother to say, is it true,
what we cannot speak about we must

pass over in silence. But what if
silence too begins to speak, or sing,
to be the hand that is no longer there.

What if death is dark as any beam
that illuminates a score of music.
Birth too. Or the want to give birth

and so be born. There is no idea
as powerful as the will to have one.
And as the orchestra gathers up

its strength beneath the hand, everything
falls the way a building falls through
blooms of dust. I live for times like that,

for beginnings, ends, the great dark hall
alive and listening, the light we only
know as light the moment that it's broken.

Ann Reisfeld Boutte

I-45 South to Galveston

The terrain flattens
like a carpet
inviting deep breaths that
snap the tension bands
constricting my chest and
summon childhood memories of
crabbing with my grandfather,
dropping baited nets
from a sun-splashed pier,
through quiet waters,
retrieving blue claws,
each catch as thrilling
as the first.
Nearing the island,
palm trees appear
in quickening sequence, promising
warm salt breezes to
caress my skin,
pastel sunsets yielding to
black velvet skies
flecked with stars the
cities never see and the most
untroubled sleep I know.

Jerry Bradley

Fishing for Snook at Sea

Moored near the pilings beneath a former highway bridge,
I pull out the Shimanos and bait—pinfish,
greenbacks, and finger mullet—and give her
her choice. "Cast into the shade," I remind,
"and use a light grip—like so."
I press her hand around mine.

We whip the rod and froth the air;
we need to keep the leaders short,
and I fix them to the braided line.
"They're made of lead, so why
don't we call them ledders?" she asks.
I pinch the flared barbs down tight.

I ask her to whisper and put
a finger to my lips. "Shhh!"
But she is tired of instructions.
"Can't we just fish?"

I tell her we'll be catching dinner soon,
but hours later without a bite she is in full pout.
She puts down her rod and asks,
"Couldn't we just buy a case of crabs instead?"

"It's a box," I tease. "A box."
She snorts and takes her line out.
fiddles with the lure on her hat.
I say again, "Don't scare the fish."
"Scare them?" she says. "Wouldn't
pulling them in the boat do that?"

First Marriage

"Dear," she said,
"if one of us were to die,
I think I'd move home to Mother."

And the compliments passed
hand to hand like combat
            or family silver.

She raised a sorry kid, he
got promoted, hit Big Spring
hard on business, sent back a card
            from the motel.

"Having wonderful time,"
he wrote.
"Wish you were her."

The Kentucky Club, Juarez

the margarita was born
just across the Santa Fe bridge

where Jack Dempsey stumbled out on all fours
where Marilyn celebrated her last divorce
where mescal still masks the thirst of desire

and lust lights their cigarettes

where Chapo moves cocaine
and young soldiers, rifles on their shoulders
languish on the corner

where the jukebox
like the killing never wants to stop

Melissa Jones Brewer

In the Meantime

West Park Baptist Church, Odessa, TX
August 19, 1979

If these pews were boats we'd row
right through the vermilion windows.
No telling how full the baptistry will get.

Tonight the men from Door of Hope Mission
have been saved, the only bath they've had
this week. Wayne, who looks like Jesus

in biker boots, has the mic, tells us
how he hitched a ride with a guy he thinks
was an angel—could've tucked his wings

into his Levi's, or could've been a trucker
like he said (knowing sheep from goats
isn't Wayne's job). *But be prepared*

to entertain those angels unaware! he shouts
Amen to angels! We shout *Amen!* to Wayne
who gives it all to God. Six men file in,

line the baptistry wall, rub dark sweat
from their necks. And Brother Parker
takes each one, holds his nose, holds him

down until his skin has been soaked
enough to rise and walk in newness of life,
as the bathwater rocks, threatens to wet

the tenors' swaying backs. *Amen!* to filthy men
made clean. *Amen!* to this Brother Parker
strong and long enough to lift six men

from the abyss, to make white waterlogged
cotton stick to their ribs. One bald man wipes
and wipes his eyes, tempting us with his salty

balm of atonement. This is no mundane
bum singing, *In that great gettin up mornin,*
fare thee well, fare thee well! We feel

his bass vibrato bouncing off the waves. *Hear*
that rollin thunder, fare thee well! We see
the bones of a grown man and how they float.

Elsie

Tonight is cold
for Odessa,
she says. Hushing
us, she moves in
close, wraps us
in her quilt.

When I was nine
like you, I had
a doll, she says.
For eight days
I had her, pretty
tin face and purple
eyes, lace dress
with pearly buttons.
Too fancy to take
outside, but I did
and dropped her.
She was crushed
by that buggy
that came by
too fast. The man
driving laughed,
that man from down
the street whose girl
played tea party
and died, poisoned
by the water.

My father died
the next day, she says,
shot when his gun
fell from the well

and went off,
killed him through
his heart. It was
cold that night.
But tonight
is colder.

She tucks the cover
in, tight beneath
our arms. This patch
by your hand,
she says, this blue
cotton piece, was cut
from the shirt
he wore when he
quit breathing.

She pats us,
whispers,
no one knows
I kept it.

Drew Buxton

Together in the Bucket (To the City)

The setting-sun-glazed hoods of dusty trucks
creeping cozy reminded me of our hangovers,
spread out in the Ranger,
cruising for greasy food,

but we sped past them
and 100-acre ranches cut out of pine forests.

We couldn't sit easy.
Our seats are scalding hot.

"I'm not going home," she said after the sun had left,

and downtown lights loomed.

Chantel Langlinais Carlson

Quilled in Blue

I.

Past thyme and rain on the window's
stillness, a woman's gaze
turns to blue. Quilled in blue seeped through
to vein the blood with ink
now gone dry. A woman's gaze turns
to her skin, Rorschach forms
islands and daggers and ships sail
across life lines once held
in a gypsy's palm. The bourbon
moon never tasted so
good. A woman's gaze turns to shut
ticks and stocks of time-crossed
memory. Drawn feathered. Drawn blue.

II.

I'll tell you how night feathers fly–
a crested wave rides on
the breaths of blue, taps to the beat
of the golden nib, and
leans into a whisper.

III.

My genius tired of beat boxing
in the corner, choking
on consonants I never caught.
He pulled cobwebs off his
eyelash and blew them into air
forming feathers that took
flight. I, too busy to notice,
stepped over them–now I
am ready–but never was good
at catching fireflies.
To wake the lost ghost kidnapped by
inconsistency, I
write. The corner shadows wisp–then–
only silence answers.

Judith Carson

In a Dry Season

Old men stand on covered porches,
eyes squinting at heat that moves
over brown lawns, shriveled shrubs.
They take off stained railroad caps,
wipe sweaty, balding heads
with bandanas faded to pink.
They do not flick their Lucky Strikes
out onto the drying grass, but crush
the glowing ends with calloused fingers.
And when they take their brief,
three-minute showers, they put buckets
in their tubs, catch water for peach trees,
rose bushes by the fence. Their wives
wash dishes and laundry in blue
enameled pans and carry the soapy water
outside to save tomatoes, okra, green beans.

Clouds gather every afternoon—a taunt—
and the air crackles with heat lightening.
The wind whips and pushes red dirt
and dried weeds across sidewalks and yards
where children press hard into the gusts
to ride their bikes or jump rope.
Farmers shake their heads, worry
over cotton fields and cattle, withered
sorghum, next year's mortgage on the farm.
They watch the sky, listen to the radio;
meet at feed stores or cafes to smoke,
drink coffee, talk about the weather.
Preachers lift their arms in supplication,
and congregations sing *Revive Us Again.*

Then something dark and ominous
rolls down from Oklahoma, or pushes
across New Mexico in heavy, green
clouds. First there's hail—*Dern near*
knocked Alvin Kendrick off his porch.

Then comes rain, a wall that moves
from one dry field into another, blusters
on into town, and finally covers all
of Nolan County. The radio snaps
and pops as lightning cuts the air,
and through the steady hum and buzz
a miracle is heard—*Rain for three days!*
It's gonna rain for three days! Hallelujah!
By evening old Fords and Chevys swarm
the lake—a crowd as big as October
football games at Mustang Bowl. Water
rushes over the spillway, Bitter Creek
rolling out root beer colored froth.
Men throw their hats and slap each other
on the back. Women lift their faces to the rain,
their hair hanging in strings against their cheeks,
and children—shoes still on—skip around
in the edges of the creek, while preachers
kiss their wives and almost dance, everyone
moving to the sound of rain and a jubilant
chorus of *Amen! And again, Amen!*

Oklahoma Visits Texas

You see it coming,
a red tidal wall rising
against the sky—Oklahoma
sweeping down uninvited,
seeping into cups. Outside
there's a blizzard of dirt
so thick, you can look
straight at the sun.
You breathe sand,
feel its crystals
between your teeth,
chew up Oklahoma,
spit it out.

You watch the postman
struggle house to house,
his hat cartwheeling
down the street,
always ahead of his fingers
as he chases it,
bending and stooping
like Buster Keaton
at the Saturday matinee.

The gritty cloud rolls and spills
over the entire surface of the day.
You can't get away from its sting.
But just before sunset,
when the wind begins to die,
and the curtain of dust falls
exposing sky, you sense
a sudden sharpness in the air,
an intensity of light
that wasn't there before,
and notice Texas' day
scrubbed clean
by Oklahoma's sand.

Rosemary Catacalos

Memory in the Making: A Poetics

for Lorna Dee Cervantes

Remember the tale where the maiden lets down her long, charged hair for the lover,
his climb to her tower hanging by golden threads, by the very roots of her dreams?

This is not that story, which even then was vague about who, if anyone, was saved.
No, we are just past what some call, without irony, the American Century.

At my university, students who own Beemers ride bikes into the fields for Earth
Sciences while brown men from another country bike to other fields for food.

The students remember this, the brown men that. They are not the same. I say this
as plain fact, though many hold sincerity has been cheapened in our complex age.

A little girl called Shelly weeps on her way to the school bus. She wears jellies, cheap
plastic copies of a Greek fisherman's sandal. She spoke Spanish before English,

her Salvadoran nana, both her parents at work. Pink keys, purple keychains, clank
against her turquoise backpack. She did not dream last night. Tearstained, she

watches a family of lizards careen around the bleached trunk of a dead redwood,
limbs bleached bones in the Wedgwood bowl of the sky. I can't see children

these days without asking what they'll remember of all this. Am I Shelly's
Miss Frances, strange neighbor woman who dressed me in shawls and sang

sadly in German? Whose husband, it was told, went up in flames on the Hindenburg?
How do we know what will touch a child, mark her forever? Remember the girls

in their pale summer dresses? Remember the women they became? And then there's
the memory locked in the cells, in the blood. Certainly potatoes are a kind of faith

to the Irish. Also recall Poland, someone's grandfather escaping under his mother's
skirts, this cliché all that's left of being Polish, Jewish, poor. Even so, the moment

still somewhere in the bone: potato stubble, smoke, strong smell of a woman's skirts,
becoming Catholic. Gazing at grandmother, what did she know, and how did she learn it?

And now we are everywhere and nowhere: videophones, internet. No borders
in the air, fresh blood on the ground. How to dance? Where does memory go

in all this? To work, *emplumada!* *¡A la chancla!* We wear the black velvet hat
that came with the dream, loosen our tongues with the fire of roasted *chiles*.

The Greek women of Souli danced off the cliff of their village to keep out of the hands
of the Turks. And here we are on the purple lip of the *cañon*, telling and telling, and

there's no such thing as going too near the sun. Each time and each time the first. Just
past the close of the American Century, the child's plastic keys rattle down the street.

Hayan Charara

Self-Portrait with Dog, Possum, Newspaper and Shovel

From the fence and from the possum
with the deep gash across its neck, I drag the dog.
And when, the temperature

steadily climbing, I come back close enough
to tell its left eye is punctured and its back broken,
the possum hisses.

The dog did this as a game
or else being what she is, a thing
of unthinking and sometimes violent force,

which is right for a dog.
I hear her now, tied up
behind me, growling, snarling, whimpering

for the kill, and over the possum's head
I lay the newspaper with its everyday, everywhere
reminders of always something—

a blindfold cinched, a bomb
among tomatoes and cucumbers, another animal
forever passing through our lives—

and raising the shovel high
I think this is right.
But it is also hard.

The first blow does not finish the job.
And I come down again,
which is harder.

Self-Portraits with Matchsticks and Kerosene

To a park with man-made lakes
and beaches hauled in
by truckloads
and too many people
driving circles around the canteens,
he took us and there taught me
to build a fire, to swim and along
the tent village road let me steer
his Buick.

At night
I caught fireflies
and stayed awake late, and later
I fooled around with girls
from towns with names
I'd never heard of and whose skin
looked and felt nothing
like my own.

Sprawled
across the seats on the drive back
I fell asleep
to his favorite music, the hum
of white-walled tires
and whirring air.

He was the one,
at home, who carried me
up the stairs and while we slept
checked the doors,
windows, and locks of the house
which, more than once,
with everyone in it, he tried
burning down.

Paul Christensen

Ode to My Mother

the Ursuline School on Chartres Street

"This is the doorway to God," the Latin inscription
reads over the stone gate. Inside, a wide courtyard,
once the playground where my mother raced
her friends to the far wall, and yelled when she won.

Her blue uniform lifted in the wind, and her white
shirt, crisp and spotless, glowed around her skinny arms.
She dreamed so hard, an apple landed on her plate.

Her thoughts were like crystals in a bowl,
each a fragment of a vision she couldn't finish.
Poor dear girl, if only I were not your son,
but your suitor, stopping to take your hand
and walking you away, into that bright future
you cried over and imagined with your glittering eyes.

But you grew like every girl around you,
your legs firm, your hands long and feminine,
with a cheap ring you made into a diamond.

Your hats were castoffs of your older sisters,
but on your head, in that blistered dressing mirror,
you rose above the footlights of your opera,
a high note pulling you into the rafters
of the theater, and opening the clouds to heaven.

What happened next put childish things away.
The man you gave your heart to
put it in his pocket, and slipped a wedding band
around your naked finger. Let him have you.
I have no regrets. Your life was good enough,
and mine sufficed to get me to old age.

But there, in that sun-rinsed court
where childhood lingers, I hear
your silvery cry, your mouth open
to the sky with that triumphant shout
that nothing could hold you back
from flying, and you would beat
your soft, imaginary wings and get away.

An Encounter

A raven, educated by the wilderness,
stands in the frozen daylight begging for food.
It's past noon, and Bryce Canyon is offseason.
I'm glad I'm not a raven,
perched on legs as thin as exclamation marks,
the blue-black wings folded powerfully
against his hungry sides. A wind
makes him shift his stance like a sailor
on a deck at sea, but I am on dry ground.

We are hurtling through space, as the sun
rots in the winter sky. My cabin is warm,
my wife sitting in a chair reading a book
about the birth of time, the primal scream it made.
She waits for me while I stand here
facing this fist of anger
and resentment, bending back his head
to scorch the landscape with a triumphant cry.

George David Clark

Gilapause

Tonight, like knots of pillow
lava in vanilla sand, the gila

monsters galvanize and spill
through vents to stormlight.

They blink chill, yellow eyes,
their burrows seething

until gravity unclenches
and they crawl the gray

Sonoran craterscape
like spiders on a ceiling.

Loosed and sprawled, I clutch
a buckhorn cholla by its neck

while bits of dust and gravel
billow out toward the satellites.

Saguaro chandeliers hang
in the un-electric haze.

Their sallow quill-lights flicker.
If my upper lip beads warm

tequila, stud-skinned gilas flex
their fangs. My fingernails

can only follow the little threads
of sandfall back so far

into the salty reaches
of the dry arroyo,

and beneath my dangling
a lightning-lipped darkness

swallows, swallows, swallows.

Variation on Story's End

1. Rain Falls on the Brothel of Lazar

I'm not the sheriff, but I wear a star
in blood across my duster's shoulder, rifle
in the holster on my back. A silver scar
of lightning splits the sky above Lazar
and in the dark I hear the horses shuffle.

I'm not a sheriff, but I'll wear the stars'
injunction till I see the judge disbarred.
I hear he tells our story to the brothel.
In its fleshy holster on my back my scar
remembers different: his betrayal, his cigar,
his pistol at my spine, and nothing lawful.

Still, I'm no sheriff, and to wear a star
makes me another liar. Tonight the far
hills tremble in the rain. My right hand's slothful
to the rifle's holster. On my back my scar
burns as I enter and the den's guitars
go dumb, go dead. The judge's curse is muffled.

I'm no one's sheriff, but I draw my scar
from its pale holster and I flash it like a star.

2. Passion Crime

You'll know the bishop's killer by the wine—
this latest murder isn't her debut.
You glimpsed her where the shadows intertwine

beneath the church spire and the bridge's spine,
her features blurred in that forgiving blue.
You'll know the bishop's killer by the wine:

a poisoned red on the victims' lips. Some signs
suggests the perp's a congregant, like you.
You glimpse her: where the shadows intertwine

before the altar under Christ divine,
she's stood. Tonight, confused, you stood there too.
You'll know the bishop's killer. Over wine

at home, you'll ponder the prelate's sheaf of unsigned
love notes—quite like your angel's script. On cue,
you'll glimpse her where the shadows intertwine

between the fire and lamplight. Something brines
the pinot on your tongue: your final clue.
You'll know the bishop's killer by the wine.
You'll glimpse her where the shadows intertwine.

3. The Clenching of the Minute Hand

As if our clocks mean nothing on this moon,
the sun stalls out above the rusty clouds.
The shuttle home should be arriving soon.

Insects rustle in their blond cocoons
that swell so fast to fill the black-leafed boughs
it seems the clock means nothing. On this moon
red eels swim jigsaws through the pale lagoons.
We paused to watch them wheel and thrash, but now
our shuttle home should be arriving soon
and we'll be glad to leave. The forest fumes
and shimmers. The stirring overhead grows loud.

What if the clock means nothing on this moon?
What if a minute hesitates, immune
to reason? What if here, an hour's proud?

The shuttle home should be arriving soon.
All noons dissolve. All days outlast their noons.
Yet cinching shadows choke the trees, which rouse.
Of course the clock means something, but this moon
means more. The shuttle's not arriving soon.

SuzAnne C. Cole

Grayness, Reconsidered

Gray the rough bark of cedar and oak,
gray the branches leaf-stripped by deer.
Mist silvers and cools the mornings
before melting in thick sun-blaze.

Gray the broad-winged red tail hawk
its colors bleached by strong sunlight,
climbing thermal updrafts, soaring
and circling fields of silvered fodder.

Gray the stately fox promenading,
over-sized triangular ears alertly pricked,
gorgeous tail plume slowly switching.
No pursuers, no need for tree-climbing.

Gray the eight-point buck fog-shielded;
head shifting, nostrils flaring with human scent.
Dare he drink from galvanized washtub?
There is no water in the woods;
dusty creeks reflect only day dazzle,
and all the swimming pools are fenced.
Implacable drought has shrunk plant cells,
withered their green to gray.
The yearlings nibble prickly pear fruit.
Panting, the buck stares down human menace,
bends to drink for long minutes.

Sarah Cortez

The Secret

Love whatever can save
your life. Your ballistic vest,
your razored reflexes. The
keys you rubber-banded
to keep from jingling. The
double-tied shoelaces that
won't come loose in a foot chase.
The short haircut a turd
can't grab in a scuffle
to ream your face into concrete.

Love
that your nerves are a taut
high wire balancing a lovely,
sequined lady. Live on her
narrow steel day and night, on
and off-duty. Remember that
loser you arrested years ago
may be ready to collect your life,
as he vowed he would
some day. But, mostly,

love
your gun. Practice drawing until
your arm is extruded machinery.
The big grip in your big hand
will cleave to palm, replacing all
other knowledge. Clean its high
performance parts as if you were
swabbing the chambered mysteries
of your own auricles and ventricles.

And
when you walk
the lawman's walk
into dirty danger, love
nothing, except
what will save your life.

The Engagement

I see them
in the eternal
shininess called youth.
                    Always
they are walking
on a wide sidewalk
in a sunlit cluster of white
houses, generous porches.
                    Forever
hopeful in a way
only possible
at another age.

                    That
slender girl in white
seersucker is me.
                    See,
she is still smiling
while he strolls
onto fashion plates
she didn't know
                    meant
gay, homosexual, queer.

                    Does
she want to marry this
exquisite man with photogenic
jaw and emerald eyes? It's
easy to say *Yes. Yes*
to everything he says
he wants, although he
never probes for what
all the other boys
                    want.

They are both lying, both
passionately lying. Him,
about his lust and his love.
Their complicated unwinding
and the screwing up
again and again.

Why
is she lying? Can't she consider
who he might be? She knows
each party is a hard black bead
swallowed in white bread.

Oh, they're waving goodbye—
eager for the future, not
caring if it's together
or apart.
Yet
each pauses, searches
the other's bright eyes
for the deliberate *I do.*

Jerry Craven

Waiting for Cardinal Dawn

Spring brings gifts: yellow columbine,
redbud and dewberry in newborn hours
of brushing lips and fingers feather
hushed by passion's tactile rhyme.
She shares perfume green as tourmaline
in slipping years when her gifts come together
to shield as might a canopy, a lime
shade of living leaf and high flowers
above these wrinkled hands in slipping time.

The wild horizon (pink Botswana agate
and fiery opals holding nighthawk
wings and pointed shadows) fades from light,
fades to magnolia scented Texas dark.
Big Thicket sweetgum trees
with red oak and slash pine stand
in pools of clover—all a greening storm,
all a hushed hiss exhaling night
air in breathless waiting for cardinal dawn.

This aventurine night offers
its green wisdom, and I must listen, must learn
to drop all bent, all broken stems,
curled leaves black, all flaked bark.
This living bloodstone riot of spring
will greet a sun-washed morning of dewberry,
red hydrangeas and iris golden forever—
if I can bear forever in such a temporal morn.

In Golden Ring

Stephen rubbed a golden opaled ring
bought from Burmese smugglers across Petaling
Street from the barrel where something inside flung
refuse—bits of orange peel, spiny
red husks of rambutan, mango pits,
blood-spattered shards of Styrofoam
—all flying into the wet market
gutter while Stephen rubbed his opal ring
and I listened to metallic thumping inside
the barrel, watched the flying refuse, stepped
closer in the moist Malaysian night to ask
Stephen about the mystery of the barrel.
"No mystery there." Steven breathed hot
on the opal, rubbed it with his sleeve.

Trembling over the barrel I saw wings
in a mad flutter toss blood
into the street, potato peels, fish
bones, feathers, the severed bird head
landing at my feet with avian eyes
striped blank now of living luster,
and I knew in that moment the butcher's hand
would soon lift from the killing barrel a stilled
creature, pluck and chop and wrap the flesh
(unmoving now forever) in brown paper.

"The Malay word for barrel is *tong*." Steven
nudged the killing tong with an indifferent toe
as a vendor retrieved the still corpse.
In that stuck moment I stood dumb,
washed in the vivid red of stunned memory,
the flashing numbness of my grandmother's
chopping day on a Texas farm, a day
when Grandmother asked me to chase
the running headless chicken, and I would not,
and she laughed, and Grandpa
laughed, and after that I refused
all Sunday golden fried meals—
such came the numbing memory leaping
from childhood into that wet Malaysian
night to dizzy and stagger while Stephen breathed
and rubbed the opal shining in a golden ring.

Evening Song

Your warmth in the night:
tropical sun on orchids,
perfumed crystal seas,

Cheri, windhover,
kestral of magic feathers,
come to us today,

come, leave the tangled
nighttime nest of thorns to brood
our world with warm wings,

to fly windhovers
sweeping out autumn twilight
shadows, and tell us

the horizon lights
in rose quartz cabochon pink,
in flame sapphire red.

Sherry Craven

The Pecos River

Somewhere between Balmorhea and nowhere
the Pecos runs to dry except for the trickle
of what was what won't be again.

Rusted Budweiser cans grow out of the dry dirt,
plastic diapers decorate the empty river bed,
scattered remnants of picnickers.

Here and there a clam shell braves to be,
claim its rightful place alongside flattened
grasses, dusted with dried used-to-be.

We sit on the bank and throw rocks at nothing, wishing
for a time of dancing grasses and slow-flowing water,
warming our skin in West Texas sun—the grand solace—
a touch of god on the banks of the Pecos.

Thomas Crofts

El Topo

"The desert is circular...therefore we must travel in a spiral."
–El Topo

The hero hangs back
then plunges
straight down.

His mayhem is godlike,
women and guns the flawless instruments
of his predilection,

such an exquisite hazard!
He enters upon the scene
like death on methamphetamines.

When justice has been accomplished
in the form of elaborate reprisals
and shocking exertions of the will

the avenger finds himself again
at loose ends, in the desert,
where the girl is now his hostage

He must therefore invent strange
scenarios in which
his turbulence is once again appropriate

dreamed up and then explored
with savage persistence
the way leads only to a cave

where you end up eating giant bugs
and being worshiped by a race of circus freaks
Note: the bugs
are probably hallucinogenic.

Noel Crook

Crows

What is it the crows know this first real day of fall
when the sky's gone vacuous and the air thins?
They bark on the lawn in their raucous code,

plumage blue-black smoke of a city
smoldering. Already they have performed
their daily harassment of the owl,

old hunchback in his snag in the backyard oak,
have communicated the exact coordinates
of the buff-colored cat and patrolled

the bedraggled roses where our best dogs
are buried. They wing in from Indian mounds
down in the woods, the back pasture

where slaves' headstones list in the fescue.
Last week I found a black widow fisted
and gleaming in the sandbox—scarlet hourglass

against black carapace—and this morning
over the bubbling of oatmeal, the low drone
of war on the television set, I felt it again:

that pang that comes with the changing
leaves, frail unease as the world tilts again
into winter—some forgotten drumming

in the marrow that should have me filling
the woodpile and rasping the axe.
The crows call in threes:

Watch, watch, watch. Shadows of wings,
they say, and gather the seeds.
Count the children again.

Notes from a Salt Flat Prisoner

Bonaire

On this island, love, there is nothing but black
and white—the sea's flat back that keeps us,
bleak shards of coral honed sharp as knives
by tireless wavelets. And the salt—vast,
blinding pans for us to rake. It galls
our wrists and shins like manacles.

Nothing grows here but these crystals. Even
the dark seaweed swirling in the inlets
rises on spindly legs as if to swim
away. Small black lizards whisper
names of home against the dry rocks
and we boil them for it. We are sick

of fish. All day the sun's blanched eye
seeks us, and not one rock
big enough to hide under. I am changed
by this place—like Lot's wife
I look back, reconfigure
the purple shadows in the struts of your

ribs, your tongue in my mouth like pure fire.
Here there is no holy water or sin.
Each night we bathe ourselves in brine,
lie under a black collar of sky, the spume
of white salt stars, the salt white moon,
the sting of crystals blooming on our skin.

The Horse Graveyard

Those summers before blood stickied
our thighs, chests bony as sparrows', we trekked
to the neighbor's pasture where we kept

our ponies, riding bareback till dusk,
straw-haired and feral under the wide sky—
our own 30 acres of Eden. We knew things then:

what it was to slice into green cool
of the pond down to the flat rock where we sat
cross-legged like war-chiefs; how speed

could swallow us, take us till it was all
there was, stealing our breaths, manes
stinging our cheeks. Trust, trust,

our ponies' feet sang in the tall grass.
But I should also tell how in the empty hours
we snuck to the burn-pit—kicked our horses

down the dusty road past "Keep Out"
signs until they would not budge,
tied them to branches of scrub oaks,

their nostrils flared, raw pink membranes
all dread, then rounded the corner on foot
to where dead horses lay blackened

on their sprawling pyres, the stench
of their unburned parts souring the clearing,
their hides like matted rugs. We picked our way

to the bleached bones of the long-dead, hunkered
to our job of prizing molars from their jaws
to trade at the bead seller's for turquoise rings

we'd wear to the movies on Friday nights,
our heels planted hard against the skulls
for the lurch of unsocketing.

I should tell how while we worked
the buzzards coughed and thumped
along the ground, their scorched meals

interrupted, then wheeled above us
as we trotted the shortcut through a sallow keloid
of cornfield toward the barn, our plunder

clacking in our pockets. Black wings
thrummed sluggish rhythms
we had not even thought of yet, whispered

the torpor of slow dances, slur
of too much beer, languor of hot backseats,
and the slow turns of betrayals–

how that next summer or the next
we left our ponies waiting in their field
while we went out to plumb the world.

Logen Cure

Supernova.

She asked for stars so you drove
past the end of the roads where
mesquite trees narrow the caliche path.

Your headlights illuminated stark angles
of cactuses, glinted in the wide eyes of some
lone creature—a fox?—before you killed
the engine and the desert concealed you
in its abiding darkness. Windows
down, together you faced the galaxy,
resplendent, at once immediate
and impossibly distant.

All evening, in rooms full
of strangers, her easy laughter
chased the emptiness from your chest.
Now, alone, you mirrored
the stillness of her starlit face,
partook of her silence, gave
thanks in the vast cathedral of night.

Carolyn Dahl

Carrying Our Loads

Driving at night, my car a silent capsule pulled along the freeway's string,
big rigs with great dane snouts crawl up behind me, nudge the air, snort

at bumpers like chained bulls. Cat-eyed lights rake my car's packed
interior, reveal a single me, uneasy as a paper target at a shooting range.

The drivers in frayed cowboy hats or trim Stetsons, with old-god faces
dulled with the opium of miles, don't detour from their compass

of purpose. Wanderlust is their only desire. Neither smiling
nor frowning, they grumble truck gears, pull out, wobble

my small car with their long trailers of secrets outlined in lights
like rodeo carnival rides. The drivers are guardians of roundups

I can't see: apples, aliens, oil, calves, chemicals, or radioactive
uranium. Level with wheels, I watch the revolution of tires,

the rubber braille-bumps the roads thin to flung black
curls I mistake for fallen animals. Sometimes real ones rise

from the grass—hunted deer seeking safety in no-gun zones
who grow crazy with the consistency of headlights, leap

like saints into the promise of chrome. The drivers swerve,
but in the country music of night, no one stops for shadows,

or deer bounding off into grass, though we glance in mirrors
that look back at all the shattered songs we leave behind.

Caudatorio

Fly for me again. Fill my eyes with a breast
so scarlet robins sob. Only you are photo luscious,
Richmondena Cardinalis, crowned with a crest,
body the color of mythical vampire tears,
poppies, dying stars, things kissed away.

At first, I believed you a Hibiscus blossom,
a stigmata shining in green leaves, chlorophyll
intensifying red, held to the branch with the
petite claw of my thoughts. But no flower
ever fell, then flew, blurring its own shape.

How can I call you back? If I paint my nails,
lips, cheeks red, will you come to me the way
you fly to a faithful mate, love her for her red
parts: beak, crest, tail tips, feathered wings?
And if there's a difference in the scents of

redheads, brunettes, and blondes, and if
I dye my hair red, will you seek me like
ripened fruit, or offer me the faith of
mustard seeds? Surely something mystical
propels your heart, flies your wings.

Red isn't granted without merit. If God lives in
the color red, as Rumi said, let me hold you
in my hand. Be my pope's holy slipper,
the fluttering hem of a cardinal's caudatorio.
You, my high priest of direction, my red prayer.

Chip Dameron

Rambling Stories

As we walked one winter morning
through your neighborhood and took
the new hike and bike trail
toward downtown, we soon found
ourselves on a country road
in Ireland, hearing McGahern's people
repeat close-held prejudices amidst
the evidence of change, and then
we hiked up a mountain village
in Gage's northwest Greece and hid
in a cave, the Nazis now gone
but teenage boys and girls forced
into comradeship, *andartes* and
andartinas sent to stop the royalists'
bullets, and next we walked along
a wet street in the Istanbul dark,
holding an unfamiliar object that
might be a clue to another of Pamuk's
Byzantine mysteries, but before
we could establish its talismanic
meaning we had reached our destination,
a small downtown café, and as Larry
the owner refilled our coffee cups
he told us stories of his days
in the Merchant Marine, his childhood
in rural western North Carolina,
his string of wives, his ninth grade
education, his thirst for books, and
his town's intolerance toward outsiders—
we'd send a couple of the boys
to kick their butts—and he smiled
as he looked across the counter
at his Mexican wife and ticked off
successes of children and step-children
in this border town that has taken
him in and let him talk and talk.

Hot Night Tale in Little Rock

Friday night, Texas League ball
at the red brick park just waiting
across the street: we skipped
our evening program, were given

three tickets by a kind local
at the gate, then settled down
with hot dogs and cold beer
and cheered on the home team

as if we knew the shortstop's
shortcomings, the pitcher's best
pitch, the way a double down
the left-field line caroms out

of the corner: on we listened
to the narrative's thwack and pop
and sizzle, the story we've known
by heart since we were kids,

sitting in the stands with our dads,
damp with humid hope, willing
for the game to go on as long
as it took to come to the right ending.

Bloomsday

Pale summer light dimples the Liffey,
Monday traffic streams along the quays,
a dozen cranes redefine the skyline,
and somewhere Molly is saying yes
again and again, the tourists clapping
and then dispersing to pubs and shops,
the locals about their ordinary rounds,
grown past the outrage and rejection,
glad now to claim the pen that sketched
their narrow consciences once, before
the smart jobs and second homes
in the west, before the Polish waitresses
and Bangladeshi porters, Joyce's
bespectacled face affixed to tee shirts
and kitchen magnets, briskly sold
for too many euros, home at last,
the annual wake one way to make
a long day recover their prodigal son.

Robin Davidson

Spell in Eleven Lines

Anemones, forsythia, the daffodils' frilled frames look back at her, a woman
under a spell.

A woman under a spell carries sprigs of pine, cedar, one rose-plum anemone to
place on a dead bird.

A dead bird is still beautiful, black and orange, claws curled in place, a shadow,
the ghost of a song.

A shadow, the ghost of a song, is what's led the woman to cedars, the unnamed
bird, the forest of night.

The forest of night is what she must watch, still, alone, outside her window, the
bird buried and waiting.

The bird buried and waiting is a sign that out of forest cedar and forsythia, her
voice will open into body.

Her voice will open into body when she breathes onto paper, noun/verb/noun/
verb, what's ancient in her.

What's ancient in her is a forest—anemones, forsythia, daffodils, cedar and pine,
the bird resurrected.

The bird resurrected, one line at a time, is a humming grown wild, the
prayerwork of poems.

The prayerwork of poems is the unsuspected salvation of a woman in need of a
forest of spells.

Forest wind, rain, silt, syllables, gather in her bones, her hands, and she leans in,
stokes the fire, begins.

William Virgil Davis

Tree Trimmers in the Neighborhood

A group of workers are sitting in a circle
up the street in a neighbor's yard. They
are eating their lunch. It is cold outside

and rain has been forecast, but they
work, inured to the weather. Yesterday
they were in our yard, eight of them

in their brightly-colored burnt-orange
coveralls, swinging through the trees,
roping their way in long loops across

the arroyo to the houses on the other side.
They sideswiped the tallest tree on the hillside,
a huge fir, which has stood sentinel-like,

halfway down the steep incline, for more
than half a century. I wonder if it will
survive? Their trucks huddle like sleepy

monsters in the middle of the street
and grind the small limbs up with lustful
glee, drowning out everything else.

In a day or two the tree trimmers will be
gone and the cats and I will roam around
these rooms again in silence and alone.

Runners

I wanted something
alive in the bare
rooms and so you gave
me a philodendron.
I put it on the heating
unit and dumped
a coffee cup of water
on it every day.
Before winter was
over it had rounded
the corner and stretched
out along the long
window by the balcony
overlooking the patio.
When we married
and moved to a new
apartment you posed
with it stretched over
your shoulders and
along the length of
both of your arms,
the excess dangling
down to the floor
and piling up. We
named it Pheidippides,
and eventually put
it in the corner on
a bookcase filled with
ancient history in our
son's room. He grew
up to run marathons.

Jennifer M. Dean

Haboob Coming West

While a great wall of red dirt rises against the blue blow
of the horizon, filling the sky like an apocalyptic coming,

an old man with work-cracked hands stands in silence
at the lip of his porch, watching its approach. He knows

there's a new word for this but can't trust himself to say it
out loud. This word didn't exist in the days when he learned

to speak. Dust storm was all they knew to call them then:
wind pushing dirt in a massive curtain, god's own shade

billowing over fields, blotting out landmarks, silting over roads,
hissing sand through cracks in window sills, and leaving

dunes blown clear from the Kansas plains. His Mama swept
and swept, dancing an endless, stooping waltz until her partner

wore her out and Pappa made mud in the hollows of his cheeks.
In those days, boys learned early how to keep their mouths sealed

against the tang of grit. Now, the old man retreats indoors, fills
his bucket with water and towels. He tromps through the house

and lays towels against door-frames and window sills, marking
each in a damp testimony of preparation.

Chris Ellery

Woman with Basket

"I do not believe in death without resurrection. If they kill me, I will be resurrected in the Salvadoran people." –Oscar Romero

The day Oscar Romero tasted the soil
of El Salvador, a woman
filled a basket with vegetables.

The sun kissed her face
and the face of the lettuce
with equal passion.

Little insects hid
in the crevices made by the leaves
and the sun could not caress them.

Yet for the time it took
the body of Oscar Romero to fall
there was no fear in all the land.

The day Oscar Romero looked up
from behind the altar, he could taste
the soil of El Salvador.

Unknown to each other, he
and the woman busy that morning with seeds
held for an instant a single thought.

They remembered the gardens of childhood,
how the stems resisted
when they pulled the squash and corn,

and how the earth stubbornly held the roots,
reluctant to lose even one
ordinary miracle.

For the Feast of the Immaculate Conception

The climax of the Sonora Caverns tour
is that moment in the Devil's Pit
when they turn the lights off to demonstrate
total darkness.

The guide had warned us. Even so
the limestone floor fell away,
a few girls screamed, and I am pretty sure
I heard Mrs. Townsend hyperventilate.

On the way back up, everyone joked
about it, and by the time we came out of the cave
we'd all been unafraid in that black world
deeper than blindness.

My eyes were barely adjusted to the sun
when Gus grabbed me by the neck, my best friend
since first grade, and whispered, I whipped it out—
right next to Doris Faraday.

Then some of us were poking around
in the gift shop buying postcards of the famous
fishtail Butterfly (it took a billion years
to grow its wings),
and some were milling

around the bus, waiting for Mrs. Townsend
to bark us aboard for the drive back to Eden High.
Jack Jackson punched Fred Sorrel's arm
with his knuckle, Judy Willis stuck out her tongue

at Jordan James, like a mole coming out
of its burrow. There is proof
how quick the body can be
in the crystalline deep

of its metamorphosis.
Moon Milk Falls, White Giants,
Palace of Angels.
Beside the bus, Doris Faraday has her arms crossed

under her breasts,
and she's talking to three of her friends,
calm as water dripping, all of them unaware
just how intently Gus and I are staring.

Sybil Pittman Estess

Mid-October

It's nearly dark but I am bathed
in sweat I'm so hot from buckets
of this work. Tomorrow no more
daylight savings time. This seems
the last hour of our wet, mosquito-
ridden heat. This citrus is not
from Key West, the Texas Valley,
Mexico, or the San Joaquin. Nom
the Texas coast has just adjusted
to ice caps melting, polar bears
homeless, oceans rising, and
growing grapefruit, oranges,
lemons here now, easily. Few
freezes anymore. So today, I
picked prickly lemons, their
small thorns irritating my skin
and me. Neighborhood trees
are so laden they fall over on
their sides before January, when
due. My three trees, new and small,
are full of their fruit. Now is the time.

Magnolia Bayou: The House

So I am on my way back
from my errand and riding
through River Oaks, the posh
Houston super-rich not mansions
but palaces being built, are
already there—quite amazing
yet not so beautiful as the pink
and purple and white and coral
azaleas in full March bloom. Then
I drive toward my own home, cross
Houston, cross the city via my route—
Alabama St—and round about Fannin

I hear on NPR that in Bay St. Louis,
Mississippi, this week a man (a Mr.
LaRound or some name like that,
who was interviewed) found an entirely
submerged house collapsed on itself
by Hurricane Katrina in Magnolia
Bayou. They pulled out an ice chest
and found an owner's name . . . she
is in Kentucky now, and her sons.
(Her man is nowhere to be found.)
So they give her some of her silver
and china and crystal—not even broken,
and she is glad. And I am now in
the ghetto and everyone is black
on the streets and speaking of houses
I am near my own. I am disoriented
thinking of a house completely
submerged in Magnolia Bayou
in Bay St. Louis and can hardly find
my way home . . . especially since
the City of Houston has torn down
eight houses at my turning point
because of the metro coming five
blocks from our house, which some
think is very good, some very bad.
I do find the turn. I turn in. I find
my house, not yet crumbled, red brick.
Not yet submerged. I do have a bayou
one block away. I do not have a River
Oaks castle or even a mansion. I have
a 1938 house, all very dry.

(Kids of various colors are playing
on the block in the March weather and
there is no wind. Just lush green now,
not hurricane season yet. Merely spring.)

Tarfia Faizullah

Sex or Sleep or Silk

You are the night
that is sometimes
a highway, fields
blurred by speed
in which wildness
doesn't stop glowing.
What do we mean
by the word *recover*?
Because I was the dome
of a hard belly over
which our mother's
coat could no longer
button, you are
the thornless half
of the cross-hatched
branch bifurcating
her flesh when I sprang
from her, small
and nettled. I am
red dirt, red dirt, red
dirt, and you are
creases of crickets
thicketing the corner
of this and every room
in which I convince
myself I'm safe.
Tangia, you are below
ground, an infinite
autumn, or in the sky,
where everyone said
you were now. I'm just
the faltering of this
flesh that fucks, bathes,
waits—sister, I'm telling
you now that I'm tired
of cataloguing loss.
I will sand glossy

the corners of this ribcage
that I empty, that empties
me. I will shame
my skin into sex
or sleep or silk.
For two decades,
your dresses hung
in an unopened closet
unworn, untouched.
I unpin myself
from each syllable
of your name. Feral
orphan, ghost bruise,
torn tether, I'm telling you
I'm never going to die.

The Distance between Fire and Ravaged Stone

I've never told the truth
about anything: not that I've often

found the defiance
of forest fires more stunning

than the pre-planned blooms
of fireworks, not the night I caught

my friend cutting her mother's sleeping
pills in half in the dark. I've tried

to accept that the lesson learned
from a plane barreling into the Pentagon

is that fire will always only ever
come close to ravishing stone,

but I still can't predict what any of us
need when we first enter the world.

The truth is, it was many years before
I understood the expanse between

stacks of planks of acres of trees
and the stacks of paper they become,

small bits of which Fermi let drift
from his fingers during the detonation

of the first atomic bomb. The truth is,
across each narrow road in Bangladesh,

men speak to each other most honestly
with their car horns. The truth is, the first

time I saw your face, it was the same day,
twenty years ago, my sister stopped breathing.

Carrie Fountain

Time to be the fine line of light

between the blind and the sill, nothing
really. There are so many things

that destroy. To think solely of them
is as foolish and expedient as not

thinking of them at all. All I want
is to be the river though I return

again and again to the clouds.
All I want is to stop beginning sentences

with *All I want*. No—no really all
I want is this morning: my daughter

and my son saying "Da!" back and forth
over breakfast, cracking each other up

while eating peanut butter toast
and raspberries, making a place for

the two of them I will, eventually,
no longer be allowed to enter. Time to be

the fine line. Time to practice being
the line. And then maybe the darkness.

Christmas in a Hotel Room

Out the window, the parking lot
and beyond that, the highway.

No doubt something important
began or ended precisely there, or

there, in that spot where the ice-white
rental car is idling neatly, clouds

of exhaust billowing up like hope,
like the hope of the Christ child, silent

in his mother's arms, finally silent
after the great yanking commotion

of birth, the donkeys steaming
outside in the moon-cold morning.

Mary, full of grace, her most radiant
and successful self, smelling the baby's

head, touching his cheek with the back
of her finger. *Finally, you're here.*

Because the windshield is fogged,
the stranger's face is obscured

behind the wheel, though I can see
the backseat is piled with gifts.

June

The black cat is always scratching
behind his ears, always slinking off

to piss in some hidden corner
of the guest room. It is both unkind

and self-congratulatory of me to feel
sympathy for people who don't

possess a sense of humor. Where
the hell do I get off, anyway?

Admitting something hardly ever
makes it better. This is something

children's shows really gloss over.
What privilege I live in, swinging last night

on Rachel's back porch swing, telling her,
It looks like one of those home shows came

and did this to your backyard while you stayed
in a hotel and worried about what they

were doing. The cabana, the fire pit,
the outdoor couches. If I could take all

the longing inside me for God and make
a backyard landscaping project

out of it, I could live a different life
and it wouldn't cost a thing, right?

John Gorman

July, West Houston

Even inland
among thin bayous in their ditches
this light is a water light.
And when it rains, the land remembers
it was once an ocean floor.

All summer the water
hangs hazing the green
of coarse grass, leathery leaf, plant spike
while sun bludgeons all color
from paint, billboard ink
almost the stones.

You know you're beaten.
This isn't only heat, it's something exponential,
Something Else—a new element
you'll learn to live or die in.

The day feathers
its airs without clearing.
You think of lovers
heat-stunned moistnesses hovering
an inch from one another's lips,
coaxing, coaxing,
their bodies oozing juice.

When the planet
turns at last, you remember
the sun is a star, a furnace
whose terrible radiance washes our walls
with silvers, lemons, the faintest, whitest blues.

The twilight
Looks back at itself from a thousand mirrored buildings
and Houston's coolest suburb, the moon,
rises beyond earth's breath.

D. A. Gray

Aubade: Monk's Pond

Before the cidered glow creates
the world again, two stumble,

measured steps of blind petitioners
demand proof and night's fingers
discover, in turns, the velvet of loam,
and cuts from sycamore root and briar,

or waking, marvel how a warm sachet
of flesh covers a valley of bone –

until the world ends
on a cold, glass pane.

Stop, she says, I haven't been born.

Murmurings of wild voices echo and unseen
feet create ripples, drumming slowly
beneath the surface. Light cuts
its hue on the whetstone of clouds,
setting water ablaze, severs
the tops of trees from the sky
who weep at their loss.

In the tears, twin branches plumb downward
and winged arbiters glide on the surface between.

Laura Quinn Guidry

Alone

Toward evening I travel
past ranches and small farms.
Alone in a field, a cow
eats the scant grass. Behind her,
dense trees curve away.

You know how it is when
just as you pass something
it catches your eye
and, then, in your mind's eye
you see it again?

It was as if all loneliness
lived in that one unremarkable cow
in her little field
her head lowered and night
already in the trees.

R. S. Gwynn

Dogwatch

The North Atlantic
March, 1944

The "happy time" is long past, and the great
Convoy steams eastward at nine knots to fill
Bellies of bombers and of boys whose fate
Will be to seek out other boys to kill.
Or be killed. Twenty-six, my father stands
The dogwatch, and he smokes and looks to sea,
Having this evening folded winning hands
And held out for the right card patiently,
Raking a future in with bills and chips.
A flash, a muffled crack, and not much more,
And where, a moment since, one of our ships
Has been, more depths of darkness than before,
And, far behind, a home, a son, a wife,
And, waiting with them to be lived, a life.

To a Wheat Penny Found in My Change

Lifted from a flapper's beaded purse,
You dribbled through Scott's fingers, whence you fell
On the shut eye of one bound for a hearse
But were plucked off before he paid in hell.

Soon you were tendered by a shabby man
To a lady proffering winesaps; next you went
To a crackpot who'd devised a flawless plan
And yearned to urge it on a President.

Stacked with nine brothers, to a dime-a-dance
Girl from an undue admirer, you became
A lucky one for Pvt. V in France,
Who flipped you to a whore who had no name.

You came back, as the bad ones always will,
To snore six decades in a Mason jar–
Released, returned now for a wrinkled bill,
Spent for these thoughts, to tell us who we are.

Albert Haley

On the Eagle Ford Shale

The sand truck thunders and rattles past
the tin-roof trailer that looks like a dozen
other broken boxes in the colonia.

She stands beneath the dangling pest strip,
putting on makeup in the mirror.
Mars, she thinks, I live on Mars.

Out front a feral hog leg has been dropped
by a roaming bobcat that came by in the night.
It will rot.

Hands on hip she inspects from the porch
the orange and blue gas flare across the dirt
road on the other side of the railroad tracks.

Hopper cars of sand roll by, car after
car filled in Wisconsin. Steel pipe arrives
from China, the men from wherever.

She's opening a dusty can of tuna fish
and spreading it on white bread
taken from a dusty wrapper.

By noon she'll be serving steaks
and big burgers to drillers and leasing agents
and cleaning dribble off their ketchup bottles.

She's got two hundred dollars in the bank
and a claim on someone working out there
beneath a derrick's midnight lights.

He tells her how the sand, magic material, goes
in the hole with acres of water and furiously
coaxes free what never could be had before.

That sand. So fine. Could be the basis of a beach
like the ones she sees in the magazines she skims
off the Dumpster behind the library.

This is better than last year. And the year before.
This is a fucking fracking boom. You breathe
the money and, like the sex, enjoy it while you can.

At the Petroleum Club

On the fiftieth floor the white gloved staff
is seating tall men and stacked hair women.
Unapologetically they arrive, looking
like they've been squeezed out of tubes.
Country club tennis tans, vague lines in faces
like paper pre-scored for cutting.

An ice sculpture, dominates the dessert
table, the curvilinear phallic shape a celebration
of the Greenland test well that came in
last week, flowing more than a thousand barrels.

Pleasant buzz at the linen draped tables.
Salads served, a different kind of oil drizzled
over pears and walnuts and arugula.
There's elbow room and political agreement
and sons who throw footballs and daughters
who cheerlead and new SUVs valet parked.

The band starts to play on the dais as the steaks
arrive, rare, medium, well, and the light jazz
is Sinatra shaking hands with kitsch, and some
of them will dance until coffee pours from the silver pot.

By now the men are warmed up, defenses down
with the whiskeys and the aperitifs and some tales
emerging of the Emirates and Venezuela
and Russia and doing business with people
who are still at the Henry Ford stage of economic
reality, which someone points out is better
than Josef Stalin and Saddam Hussein.

They slip off for cigars, Hondurans longing
to be Cubans, and the women and the band
have to get along, marking measured time
with "You Are The Sunshine of My Life," pulling out
cells, calling the sitters, we'll be a little late
leaving tonight, and one of them goes to
the row of floor-to-ceiling windows
bearing her Dolce & Gabbana bag to find
that the city twinkles its own stars all the way out
to the Ship Channel and the refineries at Bay Town.
And could it be this woman sighs, struck by the kind
of beauty constantly being sucked right out of the ground.
All of them on top of the stalk in full amazing bloom
and so few people will ever know.

Jerry Hamby

Edge of the World

On the South Rim Trail, Big Bend, hikers pause
at the edge of the world, and survey the landscape
below the Chisos. The Chihuahuan Desert stretches
south to the Rio Grande, past the Bend,
to the Sierra del Carmen in Mexico. Landlocked sailors,
they take a sight using cell phones for sextants,
arms extended to the horizon, but failing
to catch a signal, they settle for snapshots
posed on the Rim, then pick up the trail—
Boot Canyon, Pinnacles Pass, and back to the lodge.
Tonight they will dine al fresco at the Gage Hotel;
between nachos and cabrito, another round
of margaritas, they will point their iPhones skyward
and scatter their pixelated selves to the stars.

Water's Edge

The fence is rickety—warped rails
and coils of wire freed from cedar posts.
Padlocked with rusty chain, the gate
means to secure the space, an acre of earth,
cemetery on the banks of Taylor Bayou.
On this side of the fence, a cell phone tower
spears a clear blue sky, a Quonset hut
squats in dewberry brambles,
white blooms spill into an open field.
Beyond the gate tombstones tumble
into sunken plots, and down the slope
unmarked graves vanish in the thicket—
soldiers, mothers, newborns lying
east to west, slipping to the water's edge.

Allison Adelle Hedge Coke

Cotton

Standing stooped, walking rows
quicker than those dropped to knees

crawling on dry ground, kneeling,
kneebone wearing earth,
earth wearing kneebone,
neither better for the wear
on those too big, or too weak to stand.

Stoop labor in cotton
carries more weight to field end.

Cotton cupped pricked bolls
require finesse, proper pick.

Oblige ordinary people
extraordinary extreme   effort.

Grandpa Vaughan playing Pitch
with the farrier, his heart out long before
Dad was ten. Playing Pitch – cards –
while Granny and their kids

picked the fields – clean,
choked on dust, dusted themselves,

boll held green to split prongs
calling for clever

get in, pull out
without cutting fingertips wide open.

Walking on knees,
or walking bent

dust, insects, sweat
cotton, cotton, cotton –

Until the owner offered
watermelon at wind up

– if he was a good man.

Kurt Heinzelman

In This Our Neighborhood

Once known all over the city
for its offal—hock, ear, trotter, heart—
our Foodland was shortened to FKB,
then reduced to offering catfish steaks
and bottled mole sauces, and is now
the House of Redemptive Love.
The parking lot stays unusually packed.
The rest of this strip mall will, for a fee,
cash all third-party checks for a host
of discount pagers, secondhand clothes,
and day-old bread. Down the block,
next to what was once a Pay-Less Mart,
the "Pay-Less Employment Office"
has taken its sign down at last,
a kind of mercy. Sleet has stripped
the boughs of mistletoe from the crowns
of trees, strewing the ground with green snow.
In their absence, every limb's an upright
public servant, impaling trash. Crack
by crack, Johnson grass inches past
the service lines on the netless tennis court
behind the Kwik Stop. It's a love game
in the maroon, black-glassed Cadillac
idling at the corner with its mink-lined dash,
its runningboard lights flashing fuchsia.
There's a * 99c BLIZZARD * at the DQ
and there's a car window going down
at the drive-through: freakin' in the mornin'
freakin' in the evenin' (loud,
so you can feel it in your boots,
this sole music, where the footprint
of the flight path is evolving human toes
don't ya wanna get freaky with me?
Anything hanging on a wall shakes.
"It'll freeze your brain." One by one
rows of brown sacks pass out the window.
There is a sound of corks. Champagne
pops of a drive-by—or empties lobbed

like oaths onto the deserted tennis court?
You can start to smell things adrift—
the hallelujahs and the burning rings,
the barbeque, *mi corazón*, and
all the salsas of calamity.

Tony Hoagland

Because It Is Houston,

the streetlights have to take the place
usually reserved for the moon in the poem

and the traffic in the background with its roar and surge
stands in for the ocean
                    tossing wrecks like driftwood on the shore.

Because it is Houston the
tight little blond talking on her cell phone

while backing her SUV at high speed through the parking lot
is a respected citizen

and the gnarled, serpentine, yearned-out limbs of oaks
above certain shady boulevards

suggest that even ugly can be beautiful.

Because it is Houston,
a moist wind blowing from the south at dawn

carries the faint petrochemical bouquet
                                        from the landfills of our fathers
                                                    and the landfills of their fathers.
So sweet it smells!

A morning shower
has knocked down blossoms from the honeysuckle bush
                                                        into the grass
like little ivory trumpets.

Because there is no one better qualified around,
                                    because it is Houston,

you are the one who gets to kneel
upon the buckled sidewalk

and look at them in silence.

Hard Rain

After I heard "It's a Hard Rain's Gonna Fall"
played softly by an accordion quartet
through the ceiling speakers at the Springdale Shopping Mall,
then I understood: there's nothing
we can't pluck the stinger from,

nothing we can't turn into a soft drink flavor or a t-shirt.
Even serenity can become something horrible
if you make a commercial about it
using smiling, white-haired people

quoting Thoreau to sell retirement homes
in the Everglades, where the swamp has been
drained and bulldozed into a nineteen hole golf course
with electrified alligator barriers.

You can't keep beating yourself up, Billy
I heard the therapist say on television
to the teenage murderer,
About all those people you killed—
You just have to be the best person you can be,
one day at a time -

and everybody in the audience claps and weeps a little,
because the level of deep feeling has been touched,
and they want to believe that
that the power of Forgiveness is greater
than the power of Consequence, or History.

Dear Abby:
My father is a businessman who travels.
Each time he returns from one of his trips,
his shoes and trousers
are covered with blood-
but he never forgets to bring me a nice present;
Should I say something?
Signed, America.

I used to think I was not part of this,
that I could mind my own business and get along,
but that was just another song
that had been taught to me since birth-

whose words I was humming under my breath,
as I was walking thorough the Springdale Mall.

I Have Good News

When you are sick for the last time in your life,
walking around, shaky, frail with your final illness,
feeling the space between yourself and other people
grow wider and wider
like the gap between a rowboat and its dock—
you will begin to see the plants and flowers of your youth.
And they will look as new to you as they did then—
little lavender bouquets arranged in solar systems
delicate beyond your comprehension:
the dark gold buttons with the purple manes;
the swan-white throat splashed with radish-colored flecks;
the threadlike stalks that end in asterisks.
They are where you left them, by the bus stop bench;
along the chain-link fence behind the widow's house.
And you shall squat down on your haunches
and gaze at them, just as you did before.
Because this restitution of your heart is coming,
you need not fear the indignities of death and growing old.
The synagogue of weed-head will be your evidence
that every moment
is not trampled by the march of all the rest.
It doesn't matter if you end up isolated and alone,
pulling the trigger of the morphine feed
repeatedly; it doesn't matter if you die
whimpering into the railing of the hospital bed;
refusing to see visitors,
smelling your own body in the dawn.
The dark ending does not cancel out
the brightness of the middle.
Your day of greatest joy cannot be dimmed by any shame.

The traffic goes by on Shepard Avenue.
The honeysuckle vine braids in and out and in
the spokes of the abandoned bicycle.

Katherine Hoerth

The Bull Rider

In Texas towns the tongues of men all taste
the same, like sour whiskey, dust between
the teeth. I think of this as neon lights
flicker above, my elbows on the bar.
A man sits down beside me, smells of sweat
and oil fields. He tucks his hands inside
his pockets, tells his story: he was once
a god on astroturf. I've heard it all
before, another song with steel guitar.
I lean in close and whisper in his ear:

I wanna to ride a god right out this town.

He nods his head as though he understands.
I rise up from my stool and walk across
the boot scuffed floor. I mount the metal bull
that only drunken tourists ever try.
My fingers wrapped around the plastic horn,

I wave goodbye to his Aegean eyes;
the smell of smoke gives way to Padre breeze.
I kick my heels off, touch my naked toes
to froth. The metal bull between my legs
turns into flesh; the Coastal Bend recedes.

We ride all night to Crete, and I become
a woman even gods cannot resist.

Melissa Holm

Early 1990s, Fort Hood, Texas

Fathers in our town kill
or practice it for a living.

Career fighters,
pre-pardoned murderers.

When my third grade teacher
asks my class whose parents

are in the war, we all raise
our hands. On a Wednesday,

a man drives a blue pick-up
through the bricks

of a restaurant, shot
every one he could. Females
first. One boy

survived by hiding
in the dishwasher. Adults

say nothing like this
has happened before. Except,

I heard a rumor about
my classmate and her

little brother. Their mom
chased them with an ax

through the rooms
of their house and in the garage

they escaped after she hacked
a hole through the door small

enough for them to crawl out.
And down the road in Waco,

children died in a burning house
for their parent's God. My mom
says, our God will protect us
and blasts worship music

in our house, tells me if I listen closely
I will hear angels singing.

She puts on her fanciest beaded gown,
my father in dress blues.

At the military officer's ball,
the men wear war ribbons

on their chests, dressing
up their violence,

all their children at home
listening for angels.

7th Christmas

Four days before, my mother is empty
with my father's final child. Our tree is real,
is too tall for the living room, is sawed
off at the bottom by my mother who bleeds silently
in her underwear because I'm too young to tell.

There is no man here to do men's work.
There is no Santa Claus, no time for myths
only practicalities like presents wrapped
weeks ago. (I'm getting a puzzle.)
We will celebrate in the room named for living,
and if this is life, let me tell it:

My first sister, just four, tore into the gifts days ago.
She will always yearn to know what's coming to her.
My second sister is ripe, born a day late and already
unsure of this world. Mother's tongue swirls with prayers.
In this room, father created tales he willed to vanish.

Somewhere in Arabia, he waits to shoot down fighter jets,
closer to the birth of this holiday than that of his daughter.
He rides shotgun in a Patriot missile launcher. At midnight,
a human voice cracks the season's greetings over a radio.
He sweats. The ground shivers. He decides what we remember,
where in our bodies we wear our scars.

Compost

I.
At family dinner, we chomp the rows of gold teeth
from the husks I shucked in the backyard,
the corn silk losing itself in the wind, in my hair.
We save egg shells, coffee grounds, potato skins.

All of it goes in the pile with the grass clippings,
is turned and shifted by my father's hands, his shovel.
There's heat in the breakdown. Steam rises in the mornings.

My body is small. No, tiny. I am taut limbs and red anthill high
so my father hoists me on the counter to explain the spices
in the cabinet: oregano, saffron, cardamom. I draw the circle
in my head of compost, to dirt, to life, to consumption.

II.
There was sick excitement in the warm rush of platelets
to broken skin, my cells hugging the rough edges of my wound.
Beneath my childish panic is hope in the magnetism
of seeing his own blood in another being. Mustn't he love it?

After my heart, I came to him with my other organs
in my mouth but learned to say *I will chew myself for you*
or I can wound myself before you can
or I love you but I don't need you.

Seeking him is like searching for the moon in daylight.
Sometimes he's there. Loving him is break-down,
hot friction, is chemical, is all-consuming.

Chloe Honum

The Tulip-Flame

My sister's painting this: a hill, a lane
that winds around the hill, and a wide field
of tulips with a centered tulip-flame.

She rolls her brush through gray and adds the rain
in tiny flicks, glinting arrows of cold.
My sister's painting this: a hill, a lane.

Last year our mother died, as was her plan.
It's simpler to imagine something could
have intervened. The centered tulip-flame

startles the scene; the surrounding ones are plain
pastels, while this one's lit with a crimson fold.
My sister's painting this: a hill, a lane

of cobblestones, a watery terrain
of dripping flowers. Her strokes, elsewhere controlled,
flare out and fray around the tulip-flame

as if it were an accident, a stain,
a blaze in the midpoint of a wet field.
My sister's painting this: a hill, a lane,
a tulip field, and one astounding flame.

Come Back

I can't see all of any horse at once.
They weave through twilight, in and out of sight,
as the sky drains of color, enters dusk.

The barn's a bloodstain on an ivory dress,
lost in the skirt, a spiraling red kite.
I can't see all of any horse at once.

Between us there is only field and dust,
a fence and a shadow-fence. Beside me lightning
splashes the hillside, loosens it so dusk

can wring each soggy evergreen, unlace
pink threads of berries from the shrubs. I wait.
I can't see all of any horse at once.

The moon has flown and in its place a husk
clings to the sky. The horses figure eight
in single file. Through rain-sown drapes of dusk

I try to count them, climb up on the fence.
Their foreheads shine with pearly stars, ghost-lit.
I can't see all of any horse at once—
they multiply, and shiver in the dusk.

Ann Howells

Mosquitoes

Tires shush on domed macadam
beyond county maintenance—
acres of saw grass, home to crab,
brine shrimp and snake.
Those who crave solitude
seek the salt marsh.

I feel sisters come together
to help the youngest recuperate.
Two days, and old rivalries
bubble up, spoil the broth. So I
return to the point, the familiar
sulfur reek of home.

Heavy, dank air glisters
my windshield. Headlights carve
a cavern deep in country-dark;
mosquitoes swirl toward me
like snowflakes. Were I to crack
a window the car would fill
with high-pitched whine.

Hatchlings float on stagnant pools,
semi-liquid earth; black clouds
swarm at dawn and dusk. Only
the females bite—tiny furies,
striped grey on grey. Their soft bodies
bulge with blood.

Saba Husain

Epithalamium

Under the sky:
bluebonnets, grazing cattle,
rows of cypress. We took the turn
hidden from the highway.

Father's clustered boutonniere,
Mother blushing in chiffon,
like the bridesmaids.

A shuffle of white organza.

The sequestered chapel on the hill,

where the stone pews, congregation of grasses,
aisle of mists, choral winds, and you
wait for the bell to ring.

Lindsay Illich

Atiscosa

When we bowed up to each other
I was afraid

I wore you out
the same way that

caliche has wore
me out. I'm sure

on somebody's place
they have a pivot road

like the preacher says
where to repent.

There's plenty
to go around here, plenty

seguro, y claro que si.
We can pretend to be

boatpeople but that ain't
the truth. We're

hog-tied to this dirt.
Smack-dabbed, goll-durned,

like the damned Karankawas
said it was.

Calf-cradled. We surely
goodness are calf-cradled

like you are to me
and nothin' done

wore out between us.

White Room Dendrology

When you I arrived
you had lost almost everything—
your black wristwatch, both rings, the knowledge
of swallowing. In the white room
all there's left to do here
is die. Amen and amen.

The doctor arrives
with pictures of your heart
in his coat pocket. He draws
them out like folded money,
shows me the black and white
branching veins of the ventricle.

And the weeks after arrive like
the picture of your heart in my back
pocket. I come and go,
Montaigne in the purple sage.
I come and go and you
remain in the monosyllable, a sheet

tucked under your dead arm, your
twig legs kick back
the covers. You cough, and I
look in your eyes for the almost
contralto in the cough. The good
arm reaches for my hands. You
look at my wristwatch, my rings.

Yesterday was the same
losing and penance. Amen and amen.
You sway in and out, mostly out
and almost gone, and almost,
almost losing everything—
the steady wind through your chest

my fingers growing out and budding
the roots burrowing through the bed
the floor the foundation and soon
sycamore amen and amen and
all there's left to do is die.

Glynn M. Irby

Crossing the Matagorda

Dividing air from water, the sun slides
under a morning haze abeam to portside.
I switch off the Mercury 30 to drift
over bay swells in line with currents.

A northern loon settles nearby.
For all the ghostly summer voices
he channels on the star-filled lakes
of Ontario, here in winter,
he is silent.
As silent as the blue norther
shipwreck, La Belle – discovered
and extracted from this seabed
in a cofferdam
around her circled sub-surface tomb.
Between breathing and drowning,
the buoyancy of her French oak failed,
cannons, muskets, and hawk bells sank
through dark water into hushed mud.

There are places I go for silence–

places where the creeks are still
and the bitter fog sinks into gullies
next to my ancestral hedgerow,

quiet places where I hear
the pulse of blood against
the coiled cochlea in my cranium.

I re-engage the outboard engine
and swing starboard to cross-flow
my course toward Espiritu Santo.

Lucas Jacob

Listening to the Blues on a Thursday Morning

It's difficult to swallow, this
newfound old truth that birdcalls loosed
into a morning storm and borne
away with juniper seedlings
and flights of feather-thin seed husks
last, measured against time, as long

as any life lived to observe
them. How the bile rises
in protest at the one sure fact
we have. This is the nature of
the blues: not just being done
wrong, but not having time enough

to hurt. And so the players love
the rules, endless possibility
but only the twelve bars to hold
it. Just a quick chance to worry
the loss between the teeth, the bits,
like the man says, goin' down slow.

Hungarian Sonnet 1

You think that *paradicsom* is the fruit,
and fall in love again with naming. Here,
you cry, are people after my own heart,
who hang Eden and apple in one word, fat

on the tongue! But then you learn your "paradise"
is grown on a vine, and not on a branch—
a mere tomato, *száz forint* per bunch.
You comfort yourself: the early Rabbis

saw in Biblical fruit puns for desire
(citron) and destruction (carob); you note
what scholars now favor: pomegranate.
Gránátalma! It sounds to your ear

like a "soul stone." Ineffable, but hewn
down, somehow, still, and held tight in the hand.

Kathryn Jacobs

Smoke Shapes

A charcoal-finger thicket overhead
traced background etchings: tangled, smoky. Swirls
of intricate engravings underscored–

and no one noticed. Fireworks split and bled
like war-wounds (violent, messy) while we cheered
and blinked and brushed off shrapnel paperboard

and waited for eruptions. But for me
it was the backdrop: salmon pink and gold
in giant orchids (sky-sized), turning green
since there were wiggles of that color, and

I craned my neck to see around them. Scrolls
unfolded slowly, melting as I read,
and if it weren't for spangles I could see
entire hieroglyphics–gone again.

Michael Jennings

Remembering the Alamo

It seemed half the schools in the state were named Bowie or Crockett
and most of the other half either Stephen F. Austin or Sam Houston.
They were the patron saints of the only religion that mattered
and necessitated a yearly pilgrimage to the Mecca of the Alamo,
there to ponder the great sword of a knife that had made history
on some remote sandbar or other, and the tiny room its namesake
met his end in, there in his tubercular death bed to be shot through the head
more times than anyone really wanted to count, and contemplate
Crockett's portrait, his almost girlish face and long Tennessee hair
that would have gotten him laughed out of any 1950s bar
in Texas, if not killed. Of course we never imagined the true savagery
of the event, or the suspect motives of the gang of thieves
who wanted to steal a whole country pretty much in the name
of Whiteness. We were true believers. We wanted to step across
a line in the sand, face down thousands, hear our names shouted
like oaths over the blazing green battlefields of our past.

Richard E. Joines

Against Self-Expression

Clouds, cartoon round, rounder than the child's drawing,
whose referent is not clouds, not mammatus,
not cumulus, not cumulonimbus,
not altocumulus, not anything

abiding in the heavens where the bestial
little eye has yet to turn its gaze
as the mind seeks what it needs when thinking
fails, but cotton balls, which he has never seen

used for anything but making clouds, dipped,
like toes in puddles, in Elmer's Glue and stuck
to construction paper–sometimes a darker,
sometimes a lighter blue–on days spent indoors

where this is what he is told to do. Now scoops
of drooping clouds crowd in pouches of clouds,
like fields of ripe cotton bending on stalks,
heads congregating in a guillotine

for a last conversation, churned in the harvester's
relentless spindles, like chickens cornered
in the coop as the E-Z Catch plows them
under, hoovers them up, spits them through air

to pack like soft feathered eggs cartoned
in plastic bins. These clouds stack and stack like
wooly white marbles on a veined marble shelf,
and all day long we were told what to expect,

that it will be so, precisely here, yet
we did not believe, until the afternoon
itself, thoughtless, is pounded into the ground,
hail falling, falling, falling as pure sound.

Once More from the Hymnal

As when a hound hears a certain pitch, his ears
twitch and fold, his eyes worry a little
before they roll back and close, his snout will tilt,
his lips, so nearly human, curl, and then
the howling begins, so the organ's first
few notes bring the congregation to its feet.
What a friend we have rings—high lonesome
and toneless—from blond wooden pews. Faith
adds measures beyond the staff, stretches notes
the composer cut short. Better to abide
a while longer in the celestial
before heading back to the hard words of home.

Pragmatic

Maybe you should turn right around, rewind,
or just get the hell out of here, drive fast—
Vegasward—blow something up along the way.
Stop where they house the dying. Sit down among
the dripping bags. Listen to the whimpering
bastard who's about to know what it's like
to be out of this misery. Turn off
the road in Candelaria. Stare down
the caved-in mouth of an old mine at somebody
else's greed. Drive through dust until you're thick
with it. Leave the car running outside
the casino. Walk in. Announce you've taken
Akaba. Put what's left on red.

Roger Jones

Bait

Certain hot evenings those summers
my father would pull up to Jewel's red-
and-white checkered butcher shop
on the edge of town, give me a few
wrinkled dollars, and I'd go inside to buy
for us all a fresh new cow heart to use
for fish bait at the pond. I'd step
into refrigerated air, the lobby with its
counters and stools, its trio of old men
loitering in chairs to ramble hours about
typical nothings. I'd give my order
to Jewel, the decorated vet, who stood
apart listening at the register.
Hunkered and odd, he'd grimace;
I'd flinch behind his back at his
fixed eye, his distance, the grayish
pallor of hands and face. He carried
like a secret (so my father had said)
within his body the residual bones of
shrapnel from an old battle, though
no one, not even wife, could coax him
to give up what he knew. On the wall,
he kept a picture of a cow cut up
by dotted lines into shapes like countries
soldiers had been driven across weeks
as the war waned. From the gray cavernous
confines of his lobby, he turned
and disappeared with my order into
the back shop, with its odors
of cow blood and hosed concrete.
Then he'd return, and I'd hand him
my money; he'd nod a grave thank you
and heft across to me the heavy heart
wrapped up like an artifact. In both hands,
I'd take it, sheathed in its stiff
white paper, seams taped, folds
and corners thorn-crisp, and one
edge matted ever so slightly
with the moist ooze of blood.

The Bee Tree

I would like to have found the bee tree,
rumored by the previous owner
to exist somewhere on this land.
Never quite sure where it was,
he never found it himself. Nor
provided us a map, verbal or literal,
though he was sure it was there,
somewhere. Years I crashed through
tons of leaves in woods, searching
out-of-the-way places. No sign.
I was certain it would signal me
by sound, singular humming,
thousands of bees in one place,
at work, holed up in some massive log
or hickory trunk, the front split open
like a mansion door, the wood
charred by lightning or fire.

In my mind the tree still rises like legend;
its energy fills the backwoods like
unverified gossip. What I've found
are mute acres, trees, pathless
routes, groves, small growth rising
from the cedary floor in pure un-
eventfulness, while the legend hums
elsewhere, elusive, a product of pure
hearsay passed down to us over years,
owner to owner, filling our minds
with buzzing curiosity, our brains
like hives overworked with things
we want, but cannot be certain are so.

Fady Joudah

The Bean Stalk

I was twelve when I asked my older brother about the clitoris. He told me it was a structure on the outside of a woman's vagina that was the size of a chickpea. If you hold it between your fingers, he said, a woman instantly melts, and he made a soft gesture of rubbing his index finger and thumb together, as if he were dusting off flour after eating a piece of bread, or stroking the wing of a moth. He'd never seen one, I was sure of it, but I knew he was telling the truth. He'd felt at least one in the stairwell of some building that wasn't fully housed yet on the campus where we lived in Riyadh. He had a reputation for being a Don Juan, which got him in trouble with the local boys. But the size of a chickpea? When I went to medical school the dimension never left my mind. If his fingers were accurate, objective, not subject to the delirium of pleasure at fourteen, then there's only one explanation: he must have encountered a girl with clitoromegaly. A body, a cadaver had a large penis in our anatomy lab the first year of medical school, and the tiniest woman in the class, who went on to become a pathologist, could not get over the size of it. She kept saying "Look at the size of it! How can that fit?" Two years earlier, taking pre-med anatomy, when it was penis time and the cloth had been removed, I don't know why I uttered these words under my breath: "So small yet so many troubles." A classmate who was standing right behind me approached me after class to tell me she was moved by my remark. She had been a victim of rape. I was stunned. She wanted to talk. She smiled and told me that she lived in a house in the middle of Nowhere Road, in Athens, Georgia.

Mimesis

My daughter
                    wouldn't hurt a spider
That had nested
Between her bicycle handles
For two weeks
She waited
Until it left of its own accord

If you tear down the web I said
It will simply know
This isn't a place to call home
And you'd get to go biking

She said that's how others
Become refugees isn't it?

American Gas Station

I never knew Bob.
He was older than some countries
Or a staleness between the teeth and lips,

Nothing the tongue can't sweep away
With few strokes in the middle of mountains
Which are creatures of god.

I had already seen the black-magic-
Marker sign taped to the glass door
Of his gas station,

In the god-damned Sierra,
Where I was grand and American,
Chrysler red and rented, running on empty:

Bob died last night.
And the pumps were locked,
The moon a cataract,

And the man inside, head in one hand,
Waved me away with the other.
I never knew Bob

But I imagine him bald,
Scalp showing through the mesh of his hat.
I was on vacation,

Tired of killing
Patients and saving them,
And the thought that I might walk for miles

Up mountain roads near dark
Angered me. I admit
What I wanted:

A Coke and a bag of chips.
The key to the toilet after traveling for hours.
I wanted to fall to my knees for oil.

And I admit I have, too many times,
Run on pressurized fumes that pop
Like soda when I finally reach a station.

Laurie Kolp

Whirls of Brokenness

We're on a mission
to garner unmarred

conch and coquina,
shark eyes, spotted

slipper snails
or sundials,

combing washed
up shell hash

first of March,
just before

summer's surge,
stampeding feet

crunching off
whorls, the whirls

of brokenness,
beach drift

uncomfortable,
winter soles

anxious to wade
after months

of confinement
closed-in shoes

and boots, skin
smarting each

staccato step
to shore, and then

we spot them—
sand dollars

strewn everywhere,
precious petals

bleached, a path
of richness.

Sand dollars,
unscarred

and whole,
holiness the peace

washing over us
as we kneel,

gather hope within
our pent up feelings

robbing us of love
for much too long.

Nick Lantz

Preface to the "Preface to the Poems Composed at the Orchid Pavilion"

In the late spring of 1985,
we met in the weedy lot of the Orchid Pavilion Nursery
for a little ritual purification.

Everyone came, all the half-brothers and half-sisters,
the children not yet born,
and men so old they were young again.

We sat beside the aqueduct, and gold cans of beer
floated down to us
like the lines of poems.

The end of the twentieth century hung over
us like a cartoon anvil, but the breeze
that day was a knife so sharp

you couldn't feel it cutting pieces off of you.
But then, when it's sunny, no one remembers
how quickly a century turns over.

Our mothers always said that living and dying
ran on the same business model,
that one hand washed the other.

But how to tell that to the rat whose whiskers
will be bound into the brush
that inks these very lines about him?

No, there's no use pretending the tears our mothers wept
over newborn babies and the dead
were even the same species of water.

Waiting with the Donkey

> *And Abraham said to his young men, "Stay here with the donkey; the lad and I will go yonder and worship, and we will come back to you." –Genesis 22:5*

Oh, America, you are those young fools
waiting by the donkey, while a madman
strops a knife and tells his son to look
the other way. You had a big breakfast—
sausage, egg like a temple's golden dome
on its desert of toast, but now you're bored,
so to pass the time, you take up a stick
to harry a lizard from bush to bush
while jets plow furrows in the fallow sky.
That sky belongs to every hawk you name
after yourself, and it's full of invisible
voices. Someone may be listening, or maybe
not. But then the lizard bites you, and you
pick up a rock, and things get serious.

Natasha

Oh darlink, oh darlink, won't you give up
moose and squirrel business? I am in kitchen
sharpenink knives, I am in bedroom sharpenink
myself, but you sit on couch, you watch on TV
moose pull America out of hat, recite *I wandered*
lonely as cloud. Daffodils I do not want,
my darlink. I want to be nogoodnik with you,
and you alone. Squirrel sounds like MiG plane
but laughs like boy scout, and every time,
it is your face bomb explodes in, you and I
left holdink bag. Won't you come outside,
see cloud that looks like anvil about to drop
on neighbors? I have recipe for happiness,
and it is this: forget blueprints, rubber masks,
bombs like big black cherries. Forget even
Fearless Leader and his dusty monocle.
Let us go, let us take walk and I will show you
all of dead baby birds left behind in nests,
show you prisons, tent cities, oil slicks big
as heartland. Just give me chance, my darlink,
and I will show you sometink you will really like.

Jim LaVilla-Havelin

Asa's Doves and Melons

we were hunting doves in the fields of a
friend of a friend, South Texas, dove season
guns blazing

it was a field of canteloupes, ripe, plump,
their pocky taupe and green skins
on the hard ground where doves
fell soft

he had told us the field had been picked twice already
so we could have all the melons we wanted
and, having met our limit on doves, one joker
tossed a melon into the air

cantaloupe skeet shooting—the blast blew it open
golden, pulp and seeds and all, like cracking
open the sun, like sweetness in the air
and we ate one, some

pulled the pickup over and filled the back
with heavy, ripe, warm canteloupes
while two guys kept heaving
and pulling, spraying the land and us

driving home those same fools, shooting from truck
as we rumbled home, stopped soon enough
that the game warden driving by us
missed that action—we were golden, maybe twice,
maybe even thrice

all this Asa tells me and more
across the table from Colonel J. who has his
stories from Viet Nam
and knows what analogies are

Not

same stretch of road
not so many days later
scrawny he was crossing
            alert
but today he is not

dead, spread, flat across
the road—bisected by the dotted line
not wild, not wily, not even sly
and, if death puffs the dead up,
not so scrawny anymore

this coyote is probably not
the same coyote, but the road is
this coyote, when I came upon it
even knowing the pain of loss it might cause
wished it was someone's dog, stupid
and caught by someone speeding down
            2790

but it was not
not someone's pet, not just a symbol
of the joyful wild, not my story to be
            moved at will across
            some dream of the west

on this grey February morning
not spring and not really winter
coyote splayed across the road
eyes gone out
                        not with us
                        not even with
                        himself

Shed

for Ward and Jeanie Sanders

the shed sheds
its back wall
simple collapse
simple as
that

that
I see it only
as an enlarged
        Cornell box
a walk-in cabinet
        of curiosities
just means

I haven't had to knock
down or out wasps'
            nests
haven't tried to use
            saws and nails
          tools and hardware
for any real job

rusted out and grimy

means
I just pass it on a
cloverleaf arc
to Luckey Road
day after day

as simple as that
as simple as
any gift

Rich Levy

Moon

When I looked up at the moon last night,
white button floating on a puddle,

I loved the world. And the moon. Melon
moon. Animal moon. Trinket moon.

I am desperate for the moon to be
more than the moon, and yet in its

current gorgeous state, it will most
likely remain moon-like, and

we will continue to moon at it
and love it as the moon. Same

for the world. To love it, to not
want it to be other than

what it is—our pet planet, our dimpled
and gamey home—we must say,

fine (as if the haggling is finally
over), we'll take it "as is," parched

and wobbly—and not let on to anyone
how badly we want it, how much

the world is to us, how beloved.
O fullness, o hunk of moon,

and world below the dwindling
lamp of moon. Candle. Candleholder.

Daydream

I will die like a peach
from the inside out,

soft tissue darkening,
drying, flaking apart,

losing what sweetness it had.
There will be no remedy

for this rotting, but I won't
lose my pit to decay,

holding fast with the pink strings
of my will to a hard center—

a seed, little dancing homunculus,
its desires and secret fatigue intact.

Michael Lieberman

Speaking of Tongues

1.

Speaking of Tongues

In memory of Paul Ruffin (1941-2016)

To listen to you talk, you'd think
you never left the rural south,
its dirt farms, revival tents and pickups,
that under your Ph.D. on Faulkner
you still wore bib overalls and hunted squirrels.

Your craw chocked full of church and Bible stories,
your head, a furrow of harrowed tales and poems,
the Lord of Dis dispatched you here to Texas.
Your riff on speaking in tongues was Babel wicked:
you founded a press. Pure moxie.

It was a brilliant gambit, Paul, and we,
your authors, rolled on the floor of your asylum
and spoke in tongues of our own, the dross
of our heavens and hells spewing out.

We were mad. All of us bonkers,
mad as John Clare or Blake or Hölderlin.
I want to shake him. Do you hear me?
Crazy as Nietzsche or Celan....
And we were grateful for your shelter.

And when you nagged your stable of authors,
we felt like Arabians, not hacks inching
our drays toward a merciless nowhere.

You, you were a brilliant talker, but your genius
was to keep your mouth shut when you wrote.
You let the 'shiners and sharecroppers,

the creeps, and the sad sacks speak for you,
give their own homilies, witness the local miracles.
Whatever you believed about the creator, you weren't saying.
And when they did, you left them on their own—
withheld judgment, that was for your readers.

You smote pretension like a prophet.
And made it stick.
You cast down the rod and conjured the serpent,
and your readers believed.

Ours is a pipsqueak, self-important world,
and you skated past the worst of it. We
are baronets of an islet too small for Lilliputians.
The largeness of your vision, mysterious
and generous, you kept close.
Confession was not your style.

Paul Ruffin, rhyming you's a tough 'n:
in lieu of rites, your wrongs are here on view,
freed many years from tongues and pew.
A guess: we hold a common doubt of heaven.

Our luck has run out. And yours as well, my friend.
In the sullen entropy of loss we will not meet again.
Remembrance is the only grace that fate admits.

2.

CDC Destroys Last Known Vials of Poetry Virus

They had been sealed away in hazmat vaults
at creative writing programs
and provided in attenuated form
to the rest of us in greeting cards
and tone-deaf translations of the Bible.

And now the vials are gathered,
placed in tungsten alloy pigs, next fired
to ungodly heats and cooled, then shot
beyond earth orbit to crawl the contours
of the universe. The entropy of poetry fulfilled.

Poetry was like the plague—infectious.
It could make you crazy, eat your brain away

like syphilis or amoebas, much worse than masturbation.
Like Marburg or Ebola it caused an ugly death.
Like Zika your brain would come out pea sized.

People got the bug from Homer,
who poisoned the wells and oracles
in parched, miserable Greece. You had
to drink the water. What didn't kill you,
might make you wish for death.

Good riddance to bad rubbish I say,
just one more chatty Cathy wanting
our attention in our uniquely busy times,
one more way to leave a child behind,
one more reason America is godless.

3.

Some Dark Fire

I am an ingot churning in pitch—
            molten.

Some dark fire burns within me still—
            impudent, demanding.

Despoiling wayfarer—
            your unrectified signal,
            motor neuron.

Prodigal and abstemious sojourner—
            lampblack harbinger,
            harbinger of crows.

Fulgent eyeless socket—
            your unalloying flame.

Dissolving ever-present—
            evanescent everlasting.

Savage, recondite wheel-bearer—
            you presage:

Lava-wender—
  doused with caustic emollient,
    road-besotted, time-fucked.

4.

Thinking of You

It's noon and Frank has just left the Metropolitan—
on his lunch break, out for a look see. I'm thinking,
Can't be, he's on the elevator with us at the Hilton—
Frank O'Hara and an old guy in a lavender shirt
and pinstripe suit, a well-trimmed beard.
Frank's not shy, says to him, "Who are you?
You look so distinguished," while I think,
Yeah, for a geezer, and he says, "My name
is Cooper, Martin....I'm an engineer..."
"Let me guess," then Frank changes his tune,
"I died in 1966. I always wanted one, what a great gadget,
your gift to the chatty. Never thought it would happen.
I had to jot things down and use the pay phone.
What took so long with your invention, Martin?
A mobile phone! Who could have imagined?
Perfect for a telebusker like me." Frank looks
like my wife. There you go again, Frank,
upstaging Athena, channeling the missus.
Wired dude from my past, way to go!
Sorry, my friend, you're new to this gig—
the food trucks don't visit the top floor any longer.
Go back to the museum steps. Look, there,
next to the biddy with the hyacinths,
the one who draws a bead on us.

5.

What is the Hope?

The arid one confines the beast—
in a rancid cage of plenty.
Rattle the bars, demand release,
rub against the boards, dislodge the mites,
pick off the lice and spray your urine thither,
smear your feces on your face.
You are a king in chains,

exultant in your rags,
sing the siren song and we will come
with saws and pries to free you.
You are the certain hope
and we are the shorn. Envelop us.
Set your captives free,
sweet lord of stingy Eden.

Janet Lowery

Wild West

Not many poets show up to two-step
at country western clubs sprinkled like diamonds
along main drags and back streets in Houston,
but each night the poetry of spent hearts
and renewed romance circles the crowded floor
in quarter-time along the line of dance.
Heart-shaped rhinestones pasted across
the back pockets of girls' jeans sparkle like crystals;
at wrists the click of glass and gold,
at necklines a circlet of silver and stones,
moonlight crusted at eyelid and earlobe—
it's like opening night at the Houston Grand Opera.
Men's ornate belt buckles accent western shirts
tucked into pressed and creased denim,
finished off with cowboy hats and boots—
except, that is, for veteran dancers. Dressed
in un-tucked button-downs, old denim,
and sneakers re-soled for slip and slide,
they're the pros that weave partners
through the crush of couples under disco balls,
faux starlight, and mirror-studded saddles
suspended like seraphs from ceiling beams.
Wistful rhymes about Bibles and beer,
radios and rodeos, small towns, old dogs,
and dusty roads lace plaintive refrains yearning
for a world so many miles back, so many
lifetimes ago—but it's the ride of a blue slide
on a pedal-steel guitar, the plucked strings
of mandolins, banjos, and country violins
that quicken the feet yet stay the soul, like
jewel-tones struck by the hand of Orpheus.

Corey Marks

Dumb Luck

The horse—her number smudged
by sweat and thumbs nuzzling

predictable exactas
stamped in black—stumbles

at the last, run too hard, run
beyond what her ankles could bear,

and the jockey, who'd driven
her ahead of the other horses

now churning past and flinging
back rings of dust, rides

her down, out of the grace
and rush of the race and into the hoof-

torn dirt, the shit and grit
and the shudder he's lost control of . . .

Then another rush: people
flurry to the fallen animal, the jockey

is raised, stunned and still
he feels he's moving—something roils

in him, around him, under him.
Words are inconsequential

as flies. Dumb luck.
The animal won't rise.

Nearby, the winner paces,
cooling, saddled now with the reason

for the day, heavy chest
widening against his rider's approval,

each breath ragged and expendable
and replaceable as the printed bets

that drift the grounds, skittering
between knuckles of grass

beneath the stands where people
stare, the ones who got it wrong,

used to seeing what doesn't come,
to wagering chances bound to be

nothing, nothing, nothing
but lost. Though someone got it right

and smacks his ticket
against his palm, exactly sure

of what it bears. He looks away
as the crowd around him cranes

and gawks into the afterlife
of chance—a white truck,

a man with an open-mouthed kit.
A needle. The hurtling world

closes like a gate.

Lullaby

I should be used to it by now, the way sparrows rill
to warning as they scatter from the tree across the street
where, third time this week, she trespasses,
scuttling through the lacework again, upward

among hollows close stitched to the pecan's heavy trunk,
branches swayed and rustling as though she's wind
passing through, or breath stirring deep in the body,
some small thing restless in its cage,

this woman who steadied herself on a cane
crossing the field below, stooped in her paces,
each new step needing the training of her eyes.

Each morning she's come, you've slept—
the way, I suppose, the newly recovered must—
in some pointless arrangement between bedclothes
and a body that lost track of what you trust your body to do.

For me, sleep's out the window, restless
as the petty rounds the sparrows cheep, their accounts
of stir and settle. Even the familiar disturbance startles me—
this time from the open page in *Birds of Europe*

and the song I wanted to hear that's always out of earshot.
The little block of prose roosting in my lap says
the singer refuses captivity, dies in its cage;

even to render the sketch the guide offers as measure,
someone broke a bird's neck and pierced its throat with wire
to bend the head into the posture of song,

the throe of a single, silent note that doesn't end.

*

Stir and settle: first their astonished calls, their quick-
flung bodies flushed into flight, and then

it's out of them, beyond them, panic descending
into that other register of calm, the woman in the tree

merely a part of the tree they settle back into, familiar
and wholly within their grasp. I wish you could see her—

though not enough to wake you—wish you could watch
the deft climb I described so poorly last night. Still,
in answer you read from the hardbound *Grimm's*

someone else read to you as a child curled in your bed,
one hand unfurled toward the broken-backed book
cupped in your mother's wider hand;

then, time came all the varied dangers lulled you
to sleep, the book set by, closed on the last sentence heard,
the last child lost, changed, preserved.

Once the book fell to the floor and splayed there,
bird with its song wrung out, I imagined I *could've* followed—
isn't that what the lover always does?—,

that in those days when you were farthest from me
I could find you, even where the hospital's florescence
lit your disheveled bed into an expanse
I hadn't known how to cross, every new thing

gone wrong with your body clear on the distance
of your half-turned face. I imagined I knew
what I didn't then, and led you back
through the briar thicketed between us:

Once, you woke rewritten with a fairytale's logic—
prick your finger and you'll bleed your body out.

*

Last night's story's stuck in the morning's craw:

Deep in a wood a girl found one tree so beautiful
she couldn't help but touch it, even though
it wasn't hers to touch. The tree belonged

to the old woman, feathered as an owl, waiting
in its branches. To teach a lesson, the old woman
changed the girl into a nightingale, placed her

in a cage in a room filled with other cages,
with other nightingales who never wanted to take up
worthless song but had, they learned, no other choice.

All night full throated complaint, but who listened?
Not the old woman asleep in her chair
dreaming of the next day's watch. Not the lover

who found the cottage after weeks of searching,
stood outside its window but couldn't tell
one song from another, couldn't recognize

his beloved's voice, couldn't guess the words
to her lament. The song was a distraction, a bramble,
O how it throttled him, snapped in his face, stung him

away from his purpose. Shut up. But the birds
wouldn't stop—Don't you know who I am?
Don't you know, don't you know?

When he found the door he would open each cage
and wring the piercing notes from every last throat.
What did he know of how the body can change?

*

But the story ends too soon, won't give up what
I want of it: what of the bodies raveled below their cages

and the old woman waking not to song but to wind
sucking at the little open doors? *Wait, wait,* what
of the lover wandered back into the forest—does he

know by now? And how do the sparrows soothe their panicked
away, away to *return, return*? How can the woman
unlace her frailty and step so cleanly out of it?

Pay attention, the world demands, but something
always stutters and blurs, and anyway I can never
get enough of what I've already gotten wrong,

what I didn't quite see, or saw, too late, the first time.
When you showed me the first speckle on your forehead,
the trio burst minutely on your cheek, I leaned close,

brushed the spots flush against your skin
and told you not to worry. *Wait and see. A rash,*
something small and already fading. A little tale
we wanted to believe, but hadn't come to the end of

by far; *this* story wanted to keep going. Your body
unstitched our trust in it, thread by thread, pocking
itself with blood that no longer knew to contain itself,

capillaries split and spilt across your face and hands
into a map of a country you'd never thought to visit.

And when I came after you, followed you
to where your body was filled with other bodies' blood,
what could I do but watch? What was I but distraction?

*

Outside, the woman leans easily against the trunk
while her cane rests below, ready to bear her back
out of whatever new surety she's found in the high limbs.

Between her clasped hands she presses two pecans
until they split. When she cracks her small mouth wide
I think for a moment she's breaking into song.

Janet McCann

After the Unitarian Service

He flies the university president
and the board of trustees around Texas
and I ask him what he flies

and he tells me so well I can see the plane
and smell it, faint gasoline
and old leather of seats,

board members getting off in Amarillo, Lubbock,
El Paso, the pilot waiting there in the cockpit
with a good book

and then I am heading out and he says
I want to tell you something
he says, Liberal Arts majors

make the best pilots, always,
but they keep sending us engineers
and they are terrible pilots, make mistakes

and crash planes
and I am wondering
as I rush to my car because I am late

what makes them good pilots, if it's
a feel they get for the air, after all that
Shakespeare, a kind of intuition

of clouds and currents, storms coming, mountains
or if it's that they're trained to take
the unknown into consideration, always,

not just the formula, the squidgy possibilities
or if some gene or trait that makes good pilots
also sends them into Liberal Arts

but all I really know is that I like
to think of them, my students, taking off,
waving their mortarboards,

knowing just how to guide their crafts aloft

Austin Seventies

and we are at our café on Sixth Street
sitting on outdoor tables leaning toward
the country singers up front, and jumping around in the back
of the whole enterprise are rats! Waiter says
he can't do anything about them so
we toss them our chips

now a poet reads about the
military-industrial complex which we hate
and will get rid of soon and we don't ever see it all
coming, these little cafes all torn down
and the big dark buildings going
up and Starbucks instead of
this place we love

all we can see is happy rats
dancing and we baptize them
with beer, we throw them
our chips

Wrong Turn

after Ambien, he drove in sleep,
eyes open but seeing the dream.
flakes of the past drifted off his tires

down the grey and black streets.
dark trees flashed silver
as he went to visit his dead father.

cars and bicycles and trains passed him
as he drove on, heading for the familiar road,
shifted gears and veered onto the bypass

amid honks and screeling brakes.
his sister chattered in the next seat
about her Easter hat and he did not hear her.

when he turned left off the highway
for the last stretch of the way home
there was no road, just a field of flowers,

winecups, primroses, tall grass
where his road used to be,
where his house used to be.

waking in the ambulance
the black blood reddening
he tried to understand and to explain.

Anne McCrady

Great House Road

Before subdivisions and trailer parks
sprang up like volunteer wheat,
this stretch of highway was his favorite
part about riding with his grandfather
back to the house after long days
of moving cows, gathering peaches
and fixing the fence along Onion Creek.
Hugging the metal curve
of the old Chevy truck door,
his skinny chin propped on his forearm
as the draft of the open window
turned his hair into a tangled halo,
he had spent the drive staring
into his grandfather's fields
of maize, the rusty seed-tops
flicking past as he listened
to the old man tell stories
of cotton gins and jenny mules
and low-water bridge crossings.
Jostled by the ruts and gullies
of a road meant for tractors,
he slipped into the sleep
of little boys not used to farm work,
slumped against the shoulder
of the only man he knew
who could tell for sure
the heft of dirt ready for planting,
the sky-color of coming rain
and the taste of grain ready
to be pulled from stalks
too proud to bend to progress.

Hunting Party

On a gunbarrel morning,
when pine branches are breaking
with ice weight, and walnuts
have frozen into marbled globes,
the men return—camoed and too cold
to joke about Southern frostbite,
as they fling a flight of mallards
into the sink to defeather.

Shaking sleet from their shoulders
and pulling mud-caked boots loose,
they unpack vests and pockets
of gum wrappers and red-paper shells,
peel off wet layers of Polartec
then cotton, as they warm up
to the idea that even torn waders
are worth the taste of duck gumbo.

Huddled around the hearth
of hot biscuits and honey,
limited out, they replay the day
as they unload their stories
to offer one another sweet mercies
for missed shots, dogs
who break early and heated lies
that, deep in the ice of winter,
brothers tell brothers,
as fathers have told sons.

Walt McDonald

Hardscrabble Nights

A road rolls past our house for miles
and doesn't curve. Surveyors aimed it,
black as a Bible and seldom used. Home on the range
is a refuge, cool rooms to harbor weapons
oiled and locked. Clouds float by to wide horizons,
heading always away. Stalks and sheaves dry up
and still they come, parades of elephants and whales,
fat clouds that billow up and fade, a circus act.
Nothing claims these fields that doesn't kill,
coyotes and bobcats mainly out of sight,
panting under hawks gliding a last patrol. At dusk,
skunks waddle up, and coyotes lope after rabbits
crouched between cactus, fur giving them away
in a breeze vinegar-sweet with mesquite,
wind straight and useful as a road. Nights,
we toss under fans stirring our blood
like sauce. We dab and grapple on the bed
like in a rain dance, sweaty even in the dark.

The Gleam of Silver Wings

After Darren's jet fell spinning
out of the Asian sky,
I learned the myth of perfect flight,

all of us Icarus, birds of a feather,
accident-prone ground pounders
riding throttled fire.

I had seen airplanes in movies
tumbling and spouting smoke
and flames from under,

but not real flesh, like Darren,
the first I knew overseas
who vanished

out of blue skies far from home,
no parachute open,
ten thousand pounds of thrust

and one of us reduced
to this, a silver matchstick
tossed indifferently away.

Night Ward

for C.M., 1891–1977

leaving the ward,
I wade light down the steps
of the hospital, moths swirling
everywhere in a school of shadows.

I leave my hands in my pockets,
hunch through wings without swatting,
the moths finning their celebration of light
like fish finding a sudden flow,

a current rich with new rains.
I remember years ago my father
leaving the wet tent before dawn,
the night air thick as mist after the shower.

Trying the door flap I would see him
already on the dock, bending
under the lantern for bait, fishing
every dawn while there was time.

Now in the dim lot away from moths
I sink into the car and stare
through glass at eight floors
of hospital, blinds drawn,

with no moths swimming the dark pool
up to the eighth floor where
my father lies, the plastic tent
drowning his bed with oxygen.

His lungs breathe in, breathe out,
struggling to be gills
Through the fathoms
I see light from his window

pale as sunshine in another
element. Starting the car
I swim up to him
and wave again goodnight.

Nick McRae

Autobiography

Between the steering wheel, a skillet, and an LCD
my life begins, snake-like, to eat itself.
I live in Texas and think sometimes of places
far from Texas, where Texas is a funny word.
All day I listen to the heater and the neighbor's ceaseless dog.
Patience is a resource I was taught to horde.

I like the predawn interstate
with its dark and chill and dearth of eyes
and intellects; I like the shifting weight
of unrolled quarters as they warm my palm
then spill across the floor.
Beneath the floor a colony of ants construct
a mausoleum for their queen.

By the time our youth feels good it is already almost over.
I admit that I love staring into mirrors,
my own face like a tintype on the cold, flat silver.
I dislike dreams, especially those remembered,
and happy dreams, the cool skin of a lost beloved, are the worst;
I prefer the common, unjust persecution.

Sometimes, awake, November, in a silent wood,
I can forget the meaning of loneliness.
Every week I nearly walk into a church.
Twice a month I call my mother,
which assuages, for a while, my guilt.

I have never, barefoot, walked into the ocean
and floated off the sand, suspended like a hanged man,
but I have split the stems of fragrant sassafras
and sucked them till my mouth felt clean again
and my words at last seemed—for a moment—
something worth not idly letting out.

Fable

Nothing ever happened in the thick-vined forest
his heart became, nothing save the freak flash fires,
the stammer of the winds the tree mass broke,

nothing save the vines not native choking out
the smaller saplings horned already with disease,
nothing save the beetles eating everything not beetle.

Nothing ever pierced the green-black canopy
that blocked out light and air and kept the final fauna
blind and weak and hungry to the point of silence.

Nowhere sweet, nowhere many-colored, nowhere
anywhere not ending. Not a leaf not curled
and withered everywhere on every split-bark branch.

And then at length there came one black-aired day
a lioness with white fur lying flat who padded
lightly through the border's thorn and shadow,

always heavy, though sliding off her hide like water.
Every bramble, every stunted stem against her fur
or curled about her tail or flattened by her paws

went stiff and gray and blew away as dust
upon the breeze that streamed in through the trail
her body made. Gray too were her eyes that peered

straight past the sickened wood and banking swirls
of dust to somewhere deeper at the forest's core.
Slowly as she pressed that way all things until then tainted

fell to dust around her, and when at last she reached
the heart of the forest of his heart that heart was barren.
Bare gray earth. Bare gray stone. Bright, clean, and cold.

Garrett Middaugh

For Love of the Game

One night at a baseball game
(a rare adventure), this muscular young fellow,
killer blonde, Ryan Phillippe on attitude,
chose to slam his shoulder into mine, maliciously.
In a stadium concourse packed with fans
in line at the concession stands,
he and another guy, appearing deep in conversation,
steered a course toward me. In the instant
before we met, out of the corner of my eye,
I saw him slyly heel his shoulder;
then with a short lunge forward and a twist
of the waist he butted my bicep as hard as he could
and walked on fast. Stopped in my tracks,
stunned, hand to my arm, turned around,
I heard the roar of the crowd and thought,
the Astros scored;
meanwhile watched the two men,
continuing their discussion, disappear into the tumult.

There was thought of going after him,
choices considered: verbal confrontation
and probable denial, or vengeance—
put an elbow in his back or trip him on the stairs
to see him tumble. Turn and walk away,
mister casual, that'll teach him to fuck
with his elders. Could I have pulled it off?
Not likely. I stared at the space where an aura
of malevolence still lingered, then let it go.
Sort of. Because obviously here I am,
over three years later, still analyzing the movement,
remembering the force he was able to put
into that crisp swing—still imagining it contravened,
returned with an ascendency of drive to the aggressor.

Terry Jude Miller

Jessica, l'artiste

kneeling at her easel
her delicate hands
transfer the world
to silent paper

light moves from
her eyes to fingers
which dance with
the brush, swirling,
twirling its horsehair
skirt in autumn's pallet

hours walk
through the night
to morning, pausing
only for a moment
while the colors dry

Bryce Milligan

Trust Steel

Here in the flux of flood and drought
that is south Texas, my Decembers
are wheelbarrows of freshly split oak.

Here, where I have the luxury of abhorring
the evening-splitting rasp and growl
of the chainsaw, I allow myself
to trust a simpler tool.

It is best when the streets have gone silent
and the heavy stroke of steel on oak resounds
house to house—
                              here, deep in this city.

The chunk and thud assumes
a natural meter and again I hear Frost
rasping out memories of all his
maple and birch woods.

And here is Hall
tucking up the leaves
against the house at Eagle Pond,
banking the cold fragile flames
that await the deeper insulation
of the silencing snow.

With each fall of my red axe their lines
rear up like the faces
of forgotten friends
and I hear a cautious halting pace
in frozen woods
I shall never call
my own.

A thousand miles to the west, Ortiz
cuts piñon, loosing a wilder smell,
preparing a different spell,

but aching
with the same ritual.

Here I cut the green oak into lengths
then let it lie a single summer.
A San Antonio August will almost
split it for you, so that
it leaps apart at the touch
of December's blade.

Summers in the Country

for Tino Villanueva

Summers in the country, I was the city boy
up from Dallas to visit the farm, up to visit
up to explore up to no good up to corrupt (those
old ladies said behind their curtains) those
country girls those twelve-year-old cowgirls
who snuck beers behind the rodeo stands and
those boys who talked about which cows were
best who wondered what the hell I found so
interesting about the damn grave yard and
why did I always have a damn book with me
and was I writing down notes to give their
damn mothers or what.
Summers in the country
I was Huckleberry looking for Jim and a river
I was Woody looking for a song and glory I was
Meg trying to tesser and Davy trying to trap
the perfect coon for the perfect hat and trying
to get it all down on a back-pocket steno pad
taking shorthand on life and getting curiouser
and curiouser about how my parents survived
this damn town at all.
Summers in the country
I drove grandpa's air conditioned tractor
while field hands bent double down the long rows
sometimes singing chopping cotton always sweating
everyone of them a philosopher of labor
a poet of the machete an Odysseus
making his way back home every one of them
knowing more about the land than I ever would
in a lifetime of summers in the country.

Wild Mustard

for Mance

Sudden sunlight steams the wild mustard,
heavy headed with the vanishing mist,
and for miles the scent makes the sodden heat
worth enduring: windows down, elbow slung
against the warm damp wind.

All along this southern highway clouds
rise out of the ground to surround treetop
islands, each mysterious just so long
as it takes the gray incensed fog to fade
into the yellow light.

One hot May morning thirty years gone
I walked these Navasota bottomlands
with old man Lipscomb: "I's up way early
for a bluesman," and he laughed at the sun.
We stood in that rich light

until Mama's sausage and biscuits
drew us inside to a day of stories
and guitar licks I would never get right—
not even understand until I smelled
wild mustard in your hair.

Jonathan Moody

Unsung

My mama hated hip-hop, but I came home
from Pryor Middle School one day & found
a Camelot Music bag hanging at the end
of a banister: inside, Geto Boys' *We Can't Be Stopped*:
a tape I'd coveted for weeks. Maybe her mind
was playing tricks on her because the album
cover featured Bushwick Bill holding an ice pack
to soothe the bullet lodged in his eye—
Willie D & Scarface, the other rap crew
members, flanking the gurney on opposite sides.

I was amazed the song entitled "Gotta Let
Your Nuts Hang" didn't induce a Grand Mal
seizure. "If that song's about what I think..."
"No, mama, *Gotta let your nuts hang*
is a 5th Ward Houston expression meaning
having the balls to say *No*": as in when the CEO
of your record label notices your right eye hanging
out of your socket & sees that as an opportune
time to snap a group photo that would cement
your status as being realer than "Real Deal" Holyfield.

Geto Boys were real: not in the sense
that they'd blast the first fool who looked
at them sideways but because their most famous
track was so personal it made me believe
they'd expressed a drug dealer's private thoughts:
fleeting moments of paranoia & suicidal ideations
written on pages of yellow legal pad paper
the music industry kept tucked
beneath bulletproof vests—the contrast
of what was considered primo product.

karla k. morton

Nothing Less

There's a young buck
who comes around in the mornings
with his friends
for Saltines;

who eats the crackers one by one
from my hand,
and who, sometimes,
lets me touch his delicate
tuft of cheek.

He only has one antler—
about six inches high,
still covered with the virgin fur
of youth.
It grows up in the center of his ears
as if to balance his head.

I have watched him
wield that one antler
better than most can wield two;

and he walks fearlessly up to this
strange beast of human
while the others just stare,

and stomps one hoof
against all dangers,
and holds his slender head high
as if to say
It is I, who am greatly made.

Of Night and Flesh

A long day of funeral arrangements,
I come back and build a fire,
and the snow begins—full fat flakes.

Stirring the fire, I think about this night,
his body turning back to ash,
remembering a story I heard years ago—

how the coyotes gather and bed down
on the south side of the crematorium
on frigid nights;
the heat of that great furnace
moving through steel and plaster
and mortar and brick,
warming the outside of the building.

He never liked the cold,
so we'll wait until spring,
and take his ashes and cast them into
his favorite place—the Sangre de Cristos.

Once you give yourself to the mountain,
you can never go back.

I think about the red coals of the fire—
so much better than the cold Earth.
I think about the smile on his face as he died.
I think about wild coyotes curled against warm brick;
his body turning to flame.

Caught

That fish must have been aghast
as I leaned in close over him,
smiling,
an odd black camera in my hands.

Look, see my reflection in his eye.

Eleven years old at the Arlington public pool,
a classmate thought it funny
to push my head under water
and hold it there.

I remember my wild thrashing,
my guttural panic
as I looked up at him
through blue water
and yellow sky;

the way he threw back his head
as he laughed;
the deep roof of his mouth;
his vicious horseshoe of teeth.

Katie Darby Mullins

First Listen, Brown Hotel

The first time I heard that song, weeping
pedal steel, soft strummed guitar, I shook,
feeling like everything broken inside me
was slowly mending. You were hours down
Highway 64, while I sat in the cold hotel
room, looking at pictures of you and our
little girl, missing the dog's warmth
on my lap. A soft, Alabama drawl filtered
out of my tinny computer speakers,

singing about the lowest moments in a man's
life, what makes him want to be sober
so much that it finally sticks. And I thought
of this man, this stranger, huddled in a corner
in some unfamiliar room, apologizing (again).
I was just killing time; that night,
small comforts meant nothing to me.

I lied.
I am still in that room, still listening that song,
trying to teach myself to know that present
becomes past quickly. I am trying to tell
myself the story of this night, even as it happens.
I am trying to learn how the singer's heartbreak
and my heartbreak come together and are sweet;
trying to understand how, with you so far away,
I can still feel your breath on my neck
and your voice in my head when I close my eyes
while the man in the speakers says *I'm sorry*
on infinite loop, so far from home.

Laurence Musgrove

Nothing

When I get in my good old car
Like an old man on a hot day
I don't turn on the radio at all
But listen to the air conditioner
Roar its hardest as I'm heading out
With my old dog in the front seat
Looking out the side window
Because there's so much out there
He hasn't already wizzed on yet
And we pull up to the drive-thru
And yell at the voice in the box
A medium ice cream cone please
That we share in the parking lot
Before it starts to melt all over
And then we drive home again
Like nothing ever happened.

My Song

I'm just a local bird.
I watch the others go south.
This is my yard and this is my tree
And this is the song that comes out of my mouth.

I'm just a local bird.
I watch the evening pink in the sky.
This is my red cat who sits on that wall
And these are my roses saying goodbye.

I'm just a local bird.
I watch the yellow fall into brown.
This is my darkness when stars say hello
And this is my house running out of sound.

I'm just a local bird.
I watch the others go south.
This is my yard and this is my tree
And this is the song that comes out of my mouth.

R. C. Neighbors

Takeoff

The slight girl stutter-steps across a field
of bluestem as she kicks a soccer ball:

the sphere, a giant's speckled egg she boots
into his mouth, white teeth so much like net.
l.l
She yips and spreads her wispy arms, like wings
to celebrate—the grass, an asphalt strip.

And then she gathers speed, wind rushing past
her sunny face, and starts, too soon, to fly.

Naomi Shihab Nye

Swerve

The dog Rosie who comes home
after nine days with something darker
in her eyes will not be able to say, exactly,
where she went and what she saw.
But the summer shifts into
another key for all who searched for her.
Now we know how many mournful dogs
sprawl exhausted in dirt
on streets called Riddle and Labor,
on the back curve by the ancient brewery,
how many empty houses,
wreckages, broken shelves,
cushionless sofas, lonely tracks,
and the two shirtless brothers
who sat on the tail of their truck
watching blankly as we circled
their block. How many bony cats,
smashed bottles. . . and the man
in a white apron who burst forth
as I coaxed his dog from a shady bush to take
a closer look, does he keep it near him
in the kitchen now? Under the swirling fan,
thinking I have my eye on it, as the unwanted dogs
limp down to the river, panting
and the next night looms.

Gardeners

Plants own themselves, my neighbor insists.

Meditating on everything once nurtured in these yards

that did not take - whose failure? What pleasure in persistence?

Pete arranges in layers, thornless cacti against deeper green.

Australian grapefruits. . . his land billows & bursts, no weeds

or empty gaps. Night air adrift with fragrance,

vine entwining tree, shivering pink rose.

How does he know exactly what to do?

Who's happiest in a pot, who poisons or heals—

but if you say, *Pete, it's brilliant!* he snaps a dried leaf.

It's ephemeral, he says. *That's what it is.*

When the massive pecan on Washington Street fell flat,

crushing the yard, removing a corner of the roof,

the family posted a sign:

Thank you for 100 years of shade.

All the Names We Will Not Know

for Adriana Corral

Before dawn, trembling in air down to the old river,

circulating gently as a new season

delicate still in its softness, rustling raiment

of hopes never stitched tightly enough to any hour.

I was almost, maybe, just about, going to do that.

A girl's thick dark hair, brushed over one shoulder

so regularly no one could imagine it not being there.

Hair as a monument. Hovering - pitched.

Beloved sister, maker of plans, main branch,

we needed you desperately, where have you gone?

Here is the sentence called No no no no no.

Come back, everything grants you your freedom,

here in the mire of too much thinking,

we drown, we drown, split by your echo.

Dave Oliphant

Amaya's 'Dixie' Notes

she works each day to
have them come out right
going over them again on
this converted upright player piano
not knowing their history from

blackface minstrel to Civil War
just the tune & when
her fingers fail to hit
the keys & rightly swing
its rhythm even Lincoln loved

its lyrics she perhaps has
heard but if they're not
forgotten the land of picked
back-breaking cotton can hardly mean
a thing to her who's

never seen a boll or
a person pine to return
to a land where he
or she was born to
endure disdain from morning on

her only concern to make
the music impressed on sheets
of paper sound happy &
properly free of any mistake
will gain her teacher's praise

Carl Palmer

Shadow Lake Snow Snakes

not the inviting cotton candy snow
scene on a holiday greeting card
or sparkling fluffy flakes floating
softly in the shaken crystal globe

these wind whipped ice shards blown
thrown stinging not sticking hurled
swirled across bare brown ground like
long white snakes slithering in the sand

Dave Parsons

Color of Mourning

She awakened to Texas summer bright
in her eyes, throwing on a new yellow
robe, she dragged her body into the kitchen
to make coffee which she dug from a deep
yellow decanter. Awareness steeps through
the heart beating perks, her eyes fall on the child's
drawing that was stuck on the refrigerator door,
a yellow duck swimming on deep dark
water under another bloody sun brimming
with amber iris—Iris, goddess of the rainbow,
adding to the litany of golden messengers, all
bringing to her mind the dress, the yellow
dress that she had given to her niece
for her fifth birthday, the sweet lemon
yellow dress that the child delighted in so
that today she was to be buried in it—the sanctuary
of the summer kitchen felt unusually cold
as she cracked a single egg, spilling
carefully the delicate yoke onto melting butter
thinking, yellow—yellow—
yellow should not feel like this.

View from the Cliffs

Nature is a Haunted House–
But Art–a House that tries to be haunted.
Emily Dickinson

At Timber Cove Inn, two hours north of San Francisco, the raccoons
come to our window after a swim in the rocky garden pools at sunset

and peer into our balcony window from the old oak tree that is twisted
and flailing away from the windy sea. They are looking for handouts

from the untold treasury of travelers: scattered pet food, an orange, perhaps
a scrap of salmon jerky—the air is crisp and rich with that nice mixture

of the bounty of human creature comforts in our encampment and the promising
poignant exotic ocean, blowing in its salted and measured breaths, offering

its own stoked and smoky light, light—bringing our polluted city minds
that sumptuous meat, the essentials for that hungriest of animals—Art.

In the mornings sleek abalone divers can be seen in the shallows far below
undulating like innocent seals fishing the jagged cliffs, spooning the rocks

for that other sweet meat—a month from now we will read news that one
of these morning swimmers will have lost his head to a great white shark—

Emily Dickinson said that a poem should take the reader's head off—
today, where the near crags drop off to the deep Pacific all along Highway 1,

great shadows are turning cold blue tones black and swirling like hunger
in its haunted aqua house, while a thousand miles away, in a makeshift studio

on the edge of the Big Thicket, an artist trades her years of working to capture
the blurred past through Realism for the oblique certainty of the Abstract, diving

again and again into her Dantesque childhood darknesses, finding red renditions
and stunting yellows, black and the uncertainty of gray—she is swirling the many

colors of the truths that had been too raw to capture on a canvas...previously too vivid
for memory's chaste channels, fits of splashing colors, violently invading the sweet

sublime of unconscious pretense—finding not *Paradiso*—but, a kind of faith—
applying the simple earthly tools of brush and fabric—fearlessly opening portals—

Austin Relativity

for Fred Hanna, Eddie Peterson, Bobby Jones:
the Barton Springs Lifeguards of the sixties.

The old flagship Night Hawk Restaurant sits at a memory axis—
just over the Colorado River Bridge where Riverside Drive crosses

South Congress running east toward the Bergstrom Air Force Base;
where, at the guarded entrance, the large painted water tank spouted

PEACE IS OUR PROFESSION, the home of Dr. Strangelove's
bombers of the sixties; and later, those chillingly beautiful aquiline

Phantom jets streaking over the emerald hill country rolls
in the seventies and eighties; this same road ran west past the lazy

hills of Barton Springs, where those stunningly free living hippie
sprites would play and lay topless, sprawled across the lush

north green banks...across from the icy blue pumping methodical
flow of the springs that fronted my guard stand, appearing

at times as bodies strewn like casualties of some insidious sun
bomb, as I sweltered in baby oil mixed with the bold blood

of iodine, squinting over small patches of zinc oxide, musing
to the radio sounds of the Stones, Dylan, the many varied

voices that pumped with steely laced drum beats a music
into the heart of our turbulent days, instilling an urgent urge

to physically act—to escape from the stagnant pools of our youth,
to dive into the current of whitewater energy of the times, swim

that dark and intoxicatingly mystery, that dangerous rushing, rushing—

Brady Peterson

Like Statues

The wounds, like the cracks on an eggshell—
my mother once described it that way, what love
does to the heart, never healed for her, never scarred
over stronger than before.

Little by little the shell was irreparably broken,
like Humpty who fell, and all the king's horses,
and all the king's men—

She left notes for me to find,
but tucked away in the back of a drawer
here and there, in a book partially read,
in the side pocket of a purse.

Why couldn't we have been happy,
she mumbled, trying to make sense of a life,
as we waited like statues in the uncomfortable
chairs of a hospital waiting room.

I leaned closer and whispered softly,
do you remember the time you peed
your pants the night you almost ran
over the armadillo.

John Poch

Cowboys vs. Texans

Last century, like angels before the world was born,
Cowboys ruled the West. Now, like angels scorned,
come the Texans to lay the black on blue.
Partner, that's not face paint. That's a tattoo.
Houston's bigger when you measure earth;
but Dallas just might circumscribe Fort Worth
and then lay claim upon America besides.
Who can seize the year? a star? these bragging rights?
A cowboy often plays the lead, the hero, loner
calling the shots, misread, in trouble with the owner.
And the symbol of a bull skull doesn't take college
to understand—they sacrifice the body. The knowledge
of good and evil goes down pretty ugly in this Western.
Arm-chaired, steady as a pump jack with that beer, Texan,
throwback-jerseyed, deep down you're old school—
an Oiler, dualies in the backfield, diesel-fueled.
Or classic silver-blue's the color of the propane hour.
Frack the whole state, and choose your power.
Know your basics, the chalk of X and O on slate.
If Emmitt Smith was free will, Earl Campbell is your fate.
Pick longevity of a consistent arm and the vain
over the new old running downhill on a level plain.
Or blitz the patriotic red, white, and black
over our Republic's model quarterback.
Have faith, the ruined knees are good for praying.
It's Sunday, after all. Who works? Who's playing?
How does the hour empowering us turn into three?
All three sides of the ball—the postgame trinity.
Michele Tafoya, tell us if you know the story
when the MVP gives God the glory:
the camera finds the other, the cloth upon his head
almost hiding the grown man crying, broken in our stead.

God in the Shape of Texas

Imagine how a thing lifeless as a caliche road
even makes meat for the crooked crow
or a necessary perpendicular walk on the Caprock
without barbed wire might have made a man
a man from the expanse. And that man post-holing
could feel freedom's labor in his molars—the cedar post
that would one day boast a meadowlark
like a trophy of Western flight.
Five strands strung hip-high help God help us,
and the triumph of the cowboy boot is up there
with the bullet. Don't laugh till you shred your palm
on a twisted star or dig your heels into the real
of a stubborn bull. Iron in the hard times may rust
but waits, patient. No one around here talks of centuries.
In January, Esperanza sobs at the Texas Proud Coin Laundry.
In February, the cranes tend to settle on last year's cotton.
In March, the John Deere green comes on like a shout, by God.

Who can resist the tiller we call sand fighter as wide
as the Second Baptist Church? With this sun, who could resist
buying a hat? Across the purblinding aluminum desolation
of the football bleachers of Paducah, Texas, the wind
howls, of course, and there goes the first big tumbleweed
to mar the new truck out front worth half the house.
You can't go far before you find some corrugated metal
leaning, leading to a brick downtown, the Masonic flourish
of God's compass hung on the one impressive building
near the stoplight. On the outskirts, some dream of a boxcar
in their own front yard, a walkway of cement pavers
in the shape of Texas leading to the porch around the side.

When even children recognize the figure of an angel
rising from the Gulf of Mexico, pan-handle headed
in humility, they pledge allegiance to her flag, under God,
the white star silver in their eager eyes, postures simple
and fixed as any town's water tower and as proud.

The County Seat of Presidio County

The County Seat of Presidio County
One thinks of boats this far from water
then goes back to just so crushing into sculpture
the rear and forward quarter panels
of three cars pasteled for half a century
by the Big Bend sun, by the windy grit,

tarantula spit, and even piercing starlight
for that singular space in the mind of art:
an abandoned barracks in afternoon's half-shadow.
Even in winter, it's a long way for the glare
to chariot his old welder across the sky.
Boyd Elder sweeps the wasps from Prada Marfa
a good twenty miles from Marfa proper.
Someone else hates that someone by accident
swept the Russian schoolhouse everyone loves
to hate. A colossal horseshoe crucified
with a ridiculous man-sized nail against the sky
casts the shadow of a sickle and hammer.
Yuccas lean for decades, and the rust on all
maybe-likes the sun. After a downpour flees
east to Alpine, it's best to shake your head
at the green that nearly tries. It didn't rain last year,
and it won't rain this year, says the mayor
to the hung-over travelers who could be artists,
and one of them writes this in a notebook
to an angel he saw late last night down the long
Judd-red counter of the convenience store,
her entire right shoulder's agave-blue agave
tattoo lit by the cash register candy bar light.
She bought cigarettes as they locked the doors.
Who could know she would come all this way
with her soft bangs, her confident nostrils,
and that utterly touchable old white sweater?
He hopes deeply she might run him over
with the land yacht of her prevailing aesthetic.

Michael G. Rather, Jr.

The Father's Prophetic Vision

Rot blooms in rust-colored tree husks
And threads itself into splintered timber.

Sparse grass grows, and bones are scattered
among the dust and dirt.

The spirit walks with me here. Its eyes
on me. I hear him say *This is a desolate*

world, empty of the Father. My feet are bare
except the dust that rises with breath

and the slow air weighs on my chest.
Suddenly, worms slide from under bark

The spirit points to the horizon
and says *Not all deserts are barren.*

Cleatus Rattan

The Best Novels are Poems

Gatsby is pure poem, so is All the Kings Men,
though Penn Warren tires a little as he tackles
St. Augustine. Still he is the spoonfull of sugar
for the free will defense. The one percent know.

However, poets come from some place
they cannot return to, though they search.
There is some plot against them, which
cannot ever be coherent, it is not reasonable.

Novelists deductively plod long distances
constructive of boundaries while poets know
something there is that doesn't love bridges
or walls or any impediment the ninety-nine

rationally require. Induction relies on those
who scale walls, leap from point to metaphoric
point in figurative manner and rarely know

characters from anything more than image.

The one percent feel their way from bridge
to bridge then sigh or smile or wipe away
a tear, refuse to turn a page till the bridge
is dry. Poets travel slowly and see where
paintings come from, listen to music few hear.

MacKenzie Regier

Ogygia, TX

To call this town an island would be lying.
If I wanted back to Ithaca, I wouldn't
have followed another man's porchlight.
No safe harbor, not a swimmer sighting land.
To call this town an island would be saying
the sea of dust between us spat me out,
but I am far from blameless. The storms
here are only dirt kicking up, and the one
that brought me, I made myself.

Maybe once I was Penelope.
I stripped miles from the states
between us using letters, phone calls,
photographs and fridge magnets.
When I stopped waking curled
toward the space where you were not,
I made to weave a shroud from the distance.
The flat, dense land would not fit
my mourning loom. A woman,
I thought myself abiding.

But I'm the one who left,
who sailed away on the ebbing grass.
Already one shoe off the boat, I searched
for some bed or kitchen undusted
with my longing for your spine,
bowstrung for my fingers' heat.
A sea nymph of the dry horizon
put a Pall Mall in my palm and spun
smoke across the hair along my forearms.
I stayed the night. I stayed one more.

House Sitting

Where your flick failed, ash fringes
the desk. The first evening, I try to dust,
but it resettles the mantle and my knuckles.
On the countertop, a cup of soap unfoamed
and lavender candle for your sheets' smell.
A pack of Camels in the cupboards, blue bowls,
a mousetrap. The cigarettes taste foul, and water
delivery has not come, so I strip my mouth
with the last of the cranberry juice. On occasion,
a distant basketball smacks pavement
from beyond blinds. Some light switches
operate nothing. I can't ask about the license
plates sheltered in the silverware drawer,
or the fridge-pinned photo of a woman
whose smile splits lipstick, coat big
against the winter. By the boxy shadow
of the shoulders bottom left, I know
it is you. I know you must be taking pictures
of her right now because she is beautiful,
a half-melted snowball clutched in her red glove.
Cold slinks in through the cat door,
and the grates blow tepid air. A cobweb,
only visible once steamed, hangs shower-
corner. You must not have seen. I leave it.

Charlotte Renk

Killing the Cormorant

Japanese fishermen would often catch fish by tying a string around a cormorant's neck, tightly enough that when he dove for a fish he could catch it, but not swallow it.

And though you've tied the string
around my neck and ankle
so long and so tight now
that I cannot dive, much less
swallow the fish to feed
your belly or mine...

and even after your hunger's
filled and the tether's
gone, I don't dive.

I fear drowning now,
and fish don't taste so good
anymore. I feel the wriggle
beneath the scale and
see the milky eye.

And though my belly
craves, and my beak
curves long toward
new waters,

I cannot lift my wings,
these black-shadowed weights,
enough to mount
the sky.

Knock and the Door Shall. . .

Like a Jesus eye peeking through a peephole,
you see her; she's standing there half naked,
round-bubbled, pounding on the door, bouncing
up and down, flapping unwings in side-straddle
hops and looking ridiculous. She's doing this
in her pink bra and panties, for crying out loud,
trying to get Jesus to let her into his Hilton suite
so they can sip Zen and green tea, burn a little
patchouli and listen to Ellington, duking it out
with Hooker and Joplin.

She gulps syncopation every chance she can.
And to do it with the Man would be wild.
Now, her friend Zee's been gone to Burleson
too damn long, and she's got to talk to somebody.
She don't really gulp syncopation,
she sips it like smooth hot Crown in a mug.
Mugs make her feel down home, kind of
aw shucks instead of *oh shit* or *bootylicious*,
which she wouldn't have said in front
of her grandma or Jesus.

Mugs remind her of a rough-hewn old table
for ten, benches flanking both sides and ends.
Grandma used to ask her to pass things like
potatoes or pepper—saying, *Thanks for the
pepper* or whatever, which was a funny way,
of getting what she was after. Grandma had faith.
But she's been gone longer than Zee.

The girl wishes He'd unlock the damn door,
unzip her brows and caress the thoughts
throbbing and lighting bad places in her brain.
This little queen of belief has been dethroned
by Katrina and a couple of blows to the belly.
And since she can't unzip her brows, she'd like
to rip her heart out, set it in the Man's hand
so he could rub it 'til it beats normal again.
You know how it is alone: mugs don't hold
enough Crown or tea to live on, so "*Hey,
she says, Thanks for opening the door, J.*"

Carol Coffee Reposa

Target Practice

Mother packed a Colt
Because she feared them,
Feared those midnight pilgrims
Stumbling through the tumbleweeds
Sweat dried on their backs
Like a second skin,
A few tortillas in a sack.

And so she lined us up
Each Saturday,
Tecate Mountain behind us
A fence line
Thirty feet in front,
Juice cans balanced
On each post.

No lunch until we shot them down
One by one
Bird's Eye logos
Centered in our sights
Heavy steel wobbly
In our hands
The trigger hard to squeeze

But we brought them down,
One by one
Shot after shot
Bullets ricocheting off the barn
Casings in the hay
We brought them down
Until one day

We saw those others, thin as twigs
Weightless as leaves
Weaving over the cattle guard
Like drunks dizzy in the morning air.
I felt the gun
Fall
To my side.

Tattoo

for Adam

My face is burned into my son
Life-size
Shades of ochre, flame and blue.
I think of needles, dyes
The artist saying things like “Raise your arm,”
“Keep still,” or “Good work isn’t cheap.
Cheap work isn’t good”
While he extracts
From muscle
Curls and bright coronas
Set around my face

But not my face,
Not my features now
Their contours drooping into time.
Instead the artist works in memory,
A crinkled photograph
Taken thirty years ago
When I was first engaged.
I smile into the future
Knowing nothing that would come
Backlight shooting rays
Into my new-permed hair.

The face that slowly surfaces
Beneath the needle
Is not mine
But his
Those untried bones, taut lines.
The artists adds another swirl
And we are canonized,
My son and I
Unlikely sainthood
Radiant
Along his spine.

Sally Ridgway

Two-Dog Night

Under the savannah cypress, my black dog hugs against me,
trusting my hands. A bat shoots its crazy twilight weaving; a jet

makes its evening susurrus. Bailey sniffs my pen, she wants to know
what I know. Rosie's blonde coat is thick and giving under my fingers.

The house floats in the pool. I might be Ava Gardner. This might
be my Night of the Iguana. The dogs make their wild silent duet,

all teeth and precision. Now the night is nearly black as Bailey.
God is in her heaven. The dappled house wavers in the pool.

The dogs kiss and lick like lovers. How good it is to have their love
around and around. Does anyone live in these houses around us?

Pool motors, dogs' gnashing. Rosie digs the sidewalk, hops a frog.
They confer. My fingers draw her fur. So thick and juicy,

how can we ever die? Pool water drips from Bailey's loose lips,
her ears fold, she pads the damp grass. Magnolia blossoms fold to sleep.

Rosie's black muzzle, her deep eyes, branchy legs. Lattice lawnchair, wet
tongue on my cheek. How can I die—now that I'm perfect as lattice-work,

supple as the house in the pool, unfolded accordion, fine straight boards.
Rosie wants to lick me there, my hands drip down her. A radio, a woman's

laughter. Rosie nibbles Bailey's neck, they play like ribbons, like China Sea
sand—ribbons of black and tan—sand from volcanoes, convulsions

of memory—that perfect black and tan here in their dingo bodies,
ears erect, tails scorpion-like. The black door sways in the pool.

Impromptu

If we hadn't been sitting on the beach-house
balcony that dark night—Gulf
wind, surf, Chopin on the radio,
Dad in his wheelchair, and me. . .

If the family next door hadn't trailed
beneath the balcony, a long silent line
out to the pitch-black beach, syncopated pails
and flashlights. . .

If they weren't the night's only light, their glowworm
ragtag file intent and silent—not my awed quiet—or the soundless
mating of the sandcrabs I'd stumbled on that afternoon,
one of the male's periscope eyes cocked perfectly over in crescendo. . .

If these lights hadn't swayed down the beach coalescing
in pattern like fireflies—allegro, adagio, glow lights expanding and
contracting—their wavery, squealing hunt game. . .
Then my father would've spent a wholly
speechless day.

"Ballet," he whispers to the wind,
hands on the railing, pulling.
He rises up to catch something—a firefly? A memory
of Mother on the beach? I'm close
beside him, knowing

Chopin wrote to an old man's last
passion, to families growing and diminishing,
a choreography of sideways crabs,
some with eyes cocked, some squealing.

José Antonio Rodríguez

Reynosa, Border City

And now the wailing city,
how it howls accordions onto alleys,
sings mugs of warm beer,
dishes brown breast and tongue.
Foster mother to all boys on buses
from dirt towns
with broken farms.

The land gives.
That was never the problem.
But white rice rains
down from the north
and nothing stays
whole anymore.

Sometimes at night
I hear the bridge buckle
with the petulant weight
of labor, hear the gun chafe
against thigh uniformed in polyester.
Holstered.
And the knowing chuckle.

Then the city cynical—a membrane
permeable, a conduit
for magic too rich for us
before the tallest wall.

Given

Given the lecture
the day before,
the room filled
with the team
of investigators
and peripherals, and
the lead agent
outlining the privileged
conversations—cleric
and parishioner,
attorney and client,
doctor and patient,
husband and wife,
I knew
the first days
would be tricky:
How to determine
in the windowless room
with the wiretap going
24/7, whether two people
were married—
the initial clue,
an easy intimacy,
until you learn
to recognize the voices.

Paul Ruffin

Burying

I found him stumbling about when the mother
died, an otherwise healthy calf, and fed him
by bottle until another cow came due, then
moved him in with her for suckling.
Third night she broke his neck.
It was a right and natural thing to do:
She reasoned, if cows can reason,
that her milk was for hers alone.
I found him barely breathing, head thrown
back, unable to rise for the bottle,
his eyes already hazing over. I could see
myself fading in them, backing into fog.
I brought the pipe down hard, twice, the
second time in malice: not for him or her,
but for the simple nature of things.
Blood came from his nose, his body
quivered. I dragged him from the barn.

The hole in the winter garden was easy, quick,
and the calf fit properly, but when the
first shovel of dirt struck his side,
he kicked, with vigor. I watched the flailing
foot strike against air. Nothing else moved.
There were no considerations: I did what
needed to be done. A few more scoops clamped
the leg and the earth stilled. I mounded
the grave and turned away, looking back once
to see that nothing heaved. I felt neither
fear nor sorrow, love nor hate. I felt
the slick handle of the shovel, slid
my thumb over its bright steel blade,
breathed deep the sharp and necessary air.

Gigging Frogs

There are some things on this earth
that may be fooled by two moons,
one still as a stone in the sky,
the other dancing. Not these frogs.
A moonlit night is not a night
for going after frogs. When your light
joins the moon, their clatter stops,
the pond goes dead: they are not fooled.

It must be done on a dark and dooming night
when yours will be the only light above
the rim of the pond. You must move
with the stealth of winter with your moon,
as slow as a stone sliding across the sky.

Then, as you see the eyes take life in
a seeming joy, moon struck, you steady
the light, aim the deadly gig, and jab
the prongs through belly or head,
swift and sure as a cottonmouth.
When you have taken all you want, you
must ice them down for the trip home,
first cutting the hind legs, still joined,
from the upper torso, skinning them
like removing too tight jeans
and laying them side by side
in the ice of your cooler,
the legs of so many lovely girls
collected by a moon struck man
who slew them for his joy.

Llano Estacado: The Naming

When Coronado and his three hundred
soldiers and six hundred Pueblo slaves
pursued El Turco across this grand plateau,
he could not have known what he had entered
until mile after trackless mile they followed
their phantom prey and found on all sides
the same stretch of grass and sky,
only at night orienting themselves, gazing
at the same stars men steer their ships by,
constellations they had known before
their ascent into a shadeless hell.

In this land of alkaline waters, broken
by sudden ravines that yawned hotly open
as if the earth would swallow them,
the plated soldiers rode, sweltering
in the merciless sun, the shimmering air.
Some fell, clattering, never to rise again,
some threw their armor aside and faced the sun.

Behind them, where nearly a thousand had passed,
the grass closed like water and all about them
was nothing but the sameness of the grassy sea.
So in time they came to cut from stunted trees
that lined dry washes poles to mark their way.
Mile after mile they drove the sticks
as they moved, stakes that leaned in the wind,
trailing out behind them, monuments to their folly,
telling them nothing of where they were going
and little of where they had been.

Mo H Saidi

The Night of the Snowfall

Snow falls gently in the Hill Country
covering the meadows and the valleys.
The sluggish streaks of smoke climb quietly
from the roofs but fail to reach the lazy clouds.

On Alamo Plaza in the heart of the night
and under the flood of lights, the flakes float
like frozen moths and glow like fireflies.
They drop on the blades of dormant grass.

They alight on the cobblestones and live awhile
in silence, they dissolve before dawn.
The wet limestone walls of the mission
glow proudly after the night of the snow fall.

Jan Seale

A *Dualism*

Why the small child wants to play Monster, I don't know.

Why he wants me to chase him around the tool shed,

his trust that running in a circle will keep him safe, I don't know.

When I stop, turn around, pause, find him under my chin,

I grab him, screech, growl, make faces. He screams delightedly.

Why the grandmother in me is delighted to oblige, I don't know.

Martha Serpas

White Dog

I do not recognize her as beautiful
but lost, a pin curl on my neighbor's

curb, of an uncertain age, too cold
for a winter in the South.

Someone, I think, should hold her.
Her eyes are brown, a swollen joint

where she's settled for pavement.
I throw a comforter over her. When

should compassion be finite?
When I give her food, she buries it.

She wedges her head between
the pickets of my iron fleur-de-lis.

At 1 a.m. I am afraid to touch her.
She is quiet, denying she is caught.

I dig her a graceful exit, neither
of us admit I am helping her.

Sometimes she startles my face
with a quick lick, flings

a stuffed raccoon above her head
and laughs. I want her to be warm,

but not in my house. Soon she is next
to me in her La-Z-Boy, clawing

at my arm. She falls asleep, then
shuffles around in the morning.

I hear her Dearfoams dragging
the hardwoods. She comes to look

at me in bed, to see if I've made coffee.
No chance she'll trot out for the paper

herself. No one gets up. I put the water on
and after another nudge I let the dog out.

Pearl Snap

Education is the answer
to our social woes, and not
the get-a-good-job-after-high-school,
but the deep plodding kind, the making-
of-many-books kind, get-everybody-
together-to-debate-the-big-questions

kind. When I'm in Walmart
and some kid dangling by the wrist
is screaming, his mom in shorts that
slice her thighs saying something
deep to him through her teeth,
her long hair smelling like she has

more than one job, I know it's not her fault.
She's carrying a combination wallet/
cigarette case with a pocket for the lighter.
Her husband—well, the father of her last two,
her divorce isn't final from her ex—
is waiting in the truck, a Ford. Her dad

had a problem with that until they went
duck hunting and worked it
all out. Her man didn't graduate
even though his junior high let
the boys go when trawling season
began, but going back got harder.

She took typing and bookkeeping
and even AP math. She says she manages
a convenience store, where you learn
how to just take on the present.
Right now she just needs
to find that pearl snap for her oldest

and why is it suddenly so dang hard
to find a boy's twelve pearl snap?
They're a few like her in every cow town.
When the copter brings a woman's
child—a certain woman of that kind—
from the parish or the county

to the city, and we all stand around
the trauma bay watching environmental services
sweep up the gauze wrap and cut clothes,
and that woman from the boonies
is still not here, driving her husband's
truck as hard and steady as she can,

I'll meet her in family consult
or stand her in the shiny hallway—
she'll go anywhere—and depending
on what the test tube intern has to say,
she'll either squat, lay her forearm
against her stomach, and loose

that first wail-groan that defies conceit,
or she'll tutor me in the language
of living in good faith, of staring
down what I have to say and
opening her mind to it, taking
it in like a nursling and knowing it

whole until the two can sleep side by side.
We tell her, *it's gonna be a long road*, and
she says, *as long as there's a road, I'm on it.*

Badlands

All over his body wolves send up a mad
chorus to the moon

seeping green
across his arms and his chest

and where his new liver floats up in him
like a mushroom's flat cap.

"I feel like I'm tripping," he says
at a pitch lower than his wife hears

and then "and I don't believe in God."
No room in that room.

So much white. So much blue.
The wolves cry the great name

into the hallway where a gurney
rolls up and down the tile

looking for someone to play catch with.
Push the wheels straight, pull the cot—

It's my job to take the heat of belief.
On Wednesday

the nurses line up for ashes
in their white Crocs

and Reeboks. Wolfman
wants God so bad

he tattoos not-God—what seems not-God—
on his skin, wants to tell me

he's afraid, that the room squeezes
time like flexible hose,

that he forgets his wife's voice,
that men come in the night

to argue with him about the nature
        of stars. There are puddles of stars above

the silver wolves on his chest. Not-God sets
        a chair near his bed.

He says thank you and lays
        a hand on the skinny arm

and with his moist stare and rough
        face tries to convey

how much he trusts the moon
        who centers the persistent stars

and how he forgets the soldier sun
        who keeps everyone blinking and quiet.

Christopher Stephen Soden

In Autumn

In autumn when the sun crosses the celestial equator,
when blazing wool plaids are buttoned and smoke laces
the afternoon air, when black leaves of jasmine tea
are steeped and daylight fails before we have found
our way home, when oats are cooked and apples crushed,
when scarfs snap free and hats evade their masters.
In autumn with its crunch and crackle, rush and tingle,
its end of careless days and flush of green, its tilt
of poles and caps and spinning yarn, its quilts and
kites and stews of sweet potatoes, turnips, and beans,
its golden deaths and ember days and altars spread
with cigarettes, flowers, cokes, and photographs,
to lure those loved we lost when Papagod got lonely.
In autumn with its reap of colors, tubers, roots,
grasses, ashes, sticks, feathery grains and squashes,
its wandering restless souls and necromancers, ghouls
and zombies and misshapen folks that emerge only after
sundown to extort confections or whatever else might
please the appetites as loot. In autumn with its oboes
and clarinets and bassoons, its barn owls and coyotes
and jack rabbits in the violet dusk, its ferris wheels
and tilt-o-whirls and stick sausages, alligator boys
and gorilla women and bumper cars and smoked turkey legs,
its drizzly runny dark liqueurs and potent libations,
Saronno, Glenlivvet, Jack Daniels, Courvoisie,
its saps of blackstrap molasses, Karo syrup, Mrs.
Butterworth's and Robitussin, its salves and balms
of ointments and rubs. In autumn with its silent
gate of slumber, its early departures and radiant longing,
Madame Butterfly and Carmen and inconsolable Pagliacchi,
its raking and heaping and piling and leaping and burning.
Autumn with its forgetting and its leaving behind
is turning, once again, turning.

Punchline

I cannot tell you why I picked
Barbra Streisand in Central Park,
the first time I bought an album,
or why I chose the lavender shirt,
or watch with leather cuff, or
I guess, what might have been

considered long hair for a 15-year-old
boy visiting Mexico for the first time.
I asked myself these questions,
though of all the queasy, melancholy
revelations, one in particular

went undetected. Not the grisly crucifixes
with unforgiving saviors, martyrs crawling
to *Our Lady of Guadalupe*, the defiant
Rivera murals, vivid with depictions
of corruption and anarchy, the rainy evenings

I spent reading (while grownups sought
refuge in rum and jazz and tobacco)
about Lenny Bruce, avant-garde bi-sexual
comic who took enemas for side effects
of mainlining smack, covered windows

with foil to block vestigial sunlight.
You wonder what you might have done,
or said, when the customs official told you
to step into a small room, where he
gingerly squeezed your crotch, watching
your response. I was puzzled but not

alarmed, figuring it was just another
guy thing, outside my realm
of the uninitiated. This was before I
understood what he thought he knew,
or why things happen in the world,
and I've got to tell you,
I still don't.

Melissa Studdard

We Are the Universe

Watching your mouth as you eat I think
perhaps an apple is the universe and your body
is an orchard full of trees. I've seen the way your leaves
cling to the ground in fall, and I noticed then
that your voice sounded soft, like feathered, drifting things
coming finally to rest. Note:
I was the core in your pink flesh. You
were hungry birds
and foxes walking though the miles of me.
You climbed, dug your nails in my bark, yanked
something loose. Don't tell me what it is.
Just keep it close.
Because I planted these rows
and rows of myself for you—
so I could lick the juice from your lips,
so I could remember
how round and hot
the promise of seed. If I could find
that orchard right now, I'd run all through the rows
of you. I'd stand in the center and twirl
until, dizzy, I fell. I'd climb high and shake
until the only thing left in you was longing,
and you'd write a poem for me. You'd say:
Your mouth is the universe. Your desire
is an orchard full of trees.

I Ate the Cosmos for Breakfast

–after Thich Nhat Hanh

It looked like a pancake,
but it was creation flattened out–
the fist of God on a head of wheat,
milk, the unborn child of an unsuspecting
chicken–all beaten to batter
and drizzled into a pan.
I brewed some tea and closed my eyes
while I ate the sun, the air, the rain,
photosynthesis on a plate.
I ate the time it took that chicken
to bear and lay her egg
and the energy a cow takes
to lactate a cup of milk.
I thought of the farmers, the truck drivers,
the grocers, the people
who made the bag that stored the wheat,
and my labor over the stove seemed short,
and the pancake tasted good,
and I was thankful.

Gary D. Swaim

Black and White Rag

"Do not play this piece fast.
It is never right to play Ragtime fast." –Scott Joplin

Let it play lentando
in Chicago's searing heat.
Treat it andantino
to Miami's brooding beat.
Syncopate the cadence,
counter every black with white.
Make them taste soulful rhythm
in my Ragtime dirge tonight.

I wrote it jeremiad
with white keys laid on black,
so let it play itself sad
the sole song in town, Jack.
It's one man on the treble
and one man on the bass,
as each plays his cleft to the color of his face.

Play appassionato,
it's wrong to play it fast.
Yea, slip it in the marrow,
slow. . .gentle to the last.
A black man's soul brought down hard
in the face of a white man's spite,
that's my syncopated score
to be settled by tonight.

Carmen Tafolla

Texas, Tejas, te...

the bones of my beloveds are baked beneath your crust
stories carved into the wood and stone like scars
dawns that never woke, parched to death
or drowned in flash floods, or lynched in flash hate,
tongues forgotten and suppressed
silenced with rope or laws or
fear for the lives of children
millennia of snakes coiled beneath the brush
heatstrokes wandering lost in *monte*, canyons, gullies,
dried-up river beds
and weather that could freeze you or could fry you
all in one *caprichoso* day, *chubascos* that could wash
your house away. Yes, this is that terrain,
of history, clash, and conquest, this sacred place
that draws our best, just to survive.
That pulls my arms to flex in strength
and sense *abrazos* in your craggy rocks,
lulling night concertos in your roar
of *chicharras* and *tecolote* hoots.
Something in my blood still runs in time to
the rolling rhythm of your rivers.
Some chord in my voice
sings still the centuries of your silt.
Yearnings in my pulse tie me to your trees,
stretch me to your open skies,
conquer me with your wild yowl,
some coyote leaping stubbornly over cactus,
howling at the moon
of your impossibilities,
challenged and
in love.

Colors sift through this dirt, lost and sighing
and somehow clearly quite immortal
as I pick up my pen,
ancestors whispering o'er my shoulder,
and take dictation,
write these poems

Larry D. Thomas

Sow

Chomping her chocolates
of fresh road kills, she swaggers
through her slop, oblivious

of the piglets she crushed
during last night's slumber,
squishing through the splits

of her thick, cloven hooves.
The last boar which tried
to straddle her fabulous girth

fractured both forelegs.
She dined on his carcass
for days, grunting in the shade.

The Red Raging Waters

For weeks on end it has rained in Texas
sending the Brazos miles beyond its banks
where it rises even now under dark Texas skies

over the wooden floor of a bottomland Baptist church,
floating creaking pews shaped with the aching buttocks
of generations, the wild Brazos rising higher yet

to the stained-glass robes of the Apostles,
soaking the feet of Jesus and lapping the elbows
of His uplifted arms, creeping up the pulpit

on whose open Bible coils a fat diamondback,
the red raging waters of the Brazos
bringing to sweet communion the serpent and the saint.

Shotguns, 1987

(oil and acrylic on canvas by John Biggers)

On the porches of cottages called "shotguns"
because all their rooms open one into the next
in a line from front to back, allowing the pellets
of a shell shot through the front door unblocked
passage through the back, stand five black women
cradling dollhouse likenesses of their cottages,

their faces resolute as carved, African masks.
The pots and tubs beside them herald the purity
of the practical, domestic acts of soap preparation,
the cooking of pork, infant bathing and even
the catching of evil. The cottages' clapboard siding
resonates with the corrugated surfaces of washboards

or the rungs of ladders ascending the rows of gables
stacked above the women in luminously outlined
triangles simultaneously two and three dimensional,
all the way to the outstretched wings of birds,
far below which, on grandma's quilt, lie railroad tracks
shimmering in the numinous geometry of the angels.

Sidney Thompson

Ecosystem

Your mother, if she can sleep, must sleep like a door
that won't stay open, wedged by pillows to keep her
propped on the hinge of her left side, to keep you left,
too, close to the heart, a metronome for sleep.

There's no crowding or kinking of the old sewer line,
the Inferior Vena Cava, which recycles breathless blood
below the waist, up along the spine, past the placenta—
the scenic route— to the right atrium. The best flow

prevents hypertension, hemorrhoids, and swelling, too,
of ankles and the already spreading feet of the exterior she.
Ultrasound shows by absence you are not a boy—you are
a half-this, half-that girl in your stylish vernix, urinating

and drinking where you swim, our 26-week-old baby fish
fountain we call Emerson. Everything in the amniotic
compost tastes delectable. Sometimes I hang my arm
around you both, my hand wedged beneath her globe,

feeling for kicks and heartbeats like hooves. Is this
how gods, not goddesses, pass time, waiting for function,
a door to open—your mother to finish the bottled water
on the night stand so I can fetch another?

Wee

Our oven game, where you, at two,
gaze into the window's reflection
and chant, "Emme Da-da, Emme Da-da,"
until I hear the call and join for chase.

You alone know why you bolt when you do
to the base you choose: your drawing table,
your TV chair, or, if ambitious and doors
don't hem, my desk chair or the bath tub.

As you nurse only with Mama,
the oven game is ours.

I doubt I'll ever see an oven again
and see only an oven's face—listen to me

wax, as if I could forget the old horror,
when I leaned over the range to stir a pot,
with you just three months in my arm,
and let your foot kiss the eye—

that delayed cry, the half-melted nail,
a singe on the little piggy that went wee,
ablaze in your favorite color and the long shape
of bread, which you love almost equal to milk.

I put the first scar on you, and you scarred
back. "More wee," we say. "More wee."

Jonathan Travelstead

Sonora Desert, Warning by Rancher

Look West from the cattle fence
to the bulkheads signifying the storm's approach.
Smoke, three hundred miles out
hangs above Los Angeles county's wildfire
like a knot's thirteenth turn or an elk hide scraped clean,
tanned in potash.

Above, thunderheads form,
sparks lighting up hiding places in steel wool
you never guessed and cannot see.

The papers say turn South
and you can see the coming tide of violence:

Beautiful dark-haired women from *los Zetas*.
Cartels from Juarez who would as soon hack off your head
as look at you. That smell of bile on the wind?
An omen auguring epidemic job loss
and *Undocumented Aliens* entering our home
through the ragged holes of fences,
our children.

Any man believes that is a fool.

Feel it now, your chest quicken
at the white skirt of cotton you see flit
between stripped Chevy Suburbans and Ford trucks
long ago scudded to a stop in dust,
their dessicated frames driven as far as momentum
and bare rims allow.

Standing as you are at the border
where two bodies like estranged lovers meet,
how could you know it came like this?

How, when it is bone dry
and a snap of light just lines up with its clatter—

one drop cratering hardpan
between chaparral and prickly-pear–
a deluge breaks and the arroyo before you floods
sluicing off your way home.

There- seeming to walk on water–
we make even the saguaro into fugitives
posed in flight.

Coyote

On a mesa near Tohono
we chocked the humvee's wheels with stones
and from there watched through binoculars
the tall, broad-shouldered native in black sweats walk two miles
south to the silver bullet trailer
parked on the Mexican side of the fence.
A window was cut out in the side of the makeshift taco stand,
a hinged plywood awning held up with a lone two-by-four.
Though we identified nothing on which
could be seen the exchange of information on routes
and patrol times, or the ridiculous gringos with their humvees
bright against the mountain in their netting,
we did not have to see his face to know
he could never side with the custodians of this country.
I remember the Mexican handed him
a Corona and chorizo in a wrapper made clear by grease,
and he stood awhile until he had finished.
Then the American-Indian took a second beer,
turned, and as he began the rutted road back to the reservation,
he stumbled on the first pothole and passed out cold,
drunk on the little he had been given,
there, in the dust of the cattle road.

Natalia Treviño

To the Medical Student with Exams

Osteology is the hardest part of anatomy,
he said pulling a human hip bone from his
stuffed leather backpack, *It's been bleached,*
he told her, flipping it, naming its parts,
now dry, struggling with the terms.

She'd been his wife then, and he added,
Each edge, curve and angle has its own name.
This complex system in his hand. He practiced.
Amazed that the one bone could have so many names
Depending on how it was turned. Names came
off his lips only to be forgotten after the test.

Finding his voice in her head was like that too,
Sampling, sifting for how he said it to her,
if he said anything. She would fill in what
she did not know. Forget what he'd convinced
her never needed saying. The walls of their apartment
had held them in that one room.

Be nice to be that bone, she thought
as she held it close to the lamp.
It once belonged somewhere else.

Years later, she could feel its white weight
in her hand. How it had been removed
from school for study. *Fossa*, she remembered –
the slick embracing cup; the perfect scoop
that allows a leg to sway, tilt—wrap
itself around another leg,

shaped by the memory of digging,
by ages of fitting one inside the together.
Something for that big test in the morning.

Joseph R. Trombatore

Piñata

I raised Banty chickens
when I was in grade school
my brother before me
had quail hunted dove
huge bullfrog legs from the
neighborhood bayou back
when the water's ran clean

but I digress

It was determined once
I started fourth grade scores
that a poultry farmer I was not
one evening Mother set the table
a feast of chicken-n-dumplings
with only my gump remaining
staring into space like a deer

in headlights

Dad decided that weekend
to give my rooster to his buddy
had a farm in Pearland chickens
large white Leghorns a harem
of hens & a fat crower
who within 5 minutes gushed red
then dead as any childhood spent

piñata

Ronja Vieth

Patterns: Black and White

When the Salsa Muse
Whores you out to hard
Rock riffs and solos
While seated on a patio

You know to blame your dress
You wore in Venice, Vicenza, Rome
Trying to rein the knight
And horse for rescue

In Louisiana and beyond. Ever
Since you dance the lack
Hook yourself to Salsa, rev
Up the Merengue and

Jive the gaps never missing
A beat to worship still
As memories seep deep
Into the fabric of the night.

Celina Villagarcia

Verano in Olmito

I.

Screen door slaps
against
weathered wood

August wind arriving
through an open
door

lazy heat rises
from this
gravel road

leading
          nowhere

II.

Muscular legs
carry
caramelo children

through rows of corn

huele como maíz
tierra y verde

thick leaves slap
against arms and necks

creased with Earth

leaving red lines
in brown skin

huele como libertad, sangre

     sweat y risas

                    ¡alegre!

Loretta Diane Walker

From the Diary of Queen Vashti: A Letter to Esther

Dear Esther:
I do not speak with the tongue of Narcissus.
My loveliness is like the wine-stained goblets
that littered the guest tables of my husband—our husband.
Vanity did not bind me to my chambers that night—
The Creator did.
He would not allow the folly of a man to soil my crown
or auction my dignity to an ogling drunk.

After the sun lifted the lid of darkness,
and the red of too much wine drained from his eyes,
Xerxes would have remembered all of those men
touching me with their stares, violating me with lust.
The strength of my resolve spared me from this shame.

Should this be the fate of a queen?
To never again feel the breath of her king
rise and fall as morning against her cheek
Morning is a false soothsayer; it blinds you to the club of pain.
When that first blow strikes your knees, shock steals your voice.

The scent of trampled olives lingers outside my window.
I miss the potters' birds, mountain goats etched in walls,
the fragrance of the palace gardens.
I have no maiden to stave off this heat
swarming around my arms.
I hear you have seven.
What favor you have found with our beloved?

Caution, my young counterpart with your lovely figure
and white dove beauty; beware of banquets.
Destruction squeezes its plump head into the belly of grapes,
it waits to be pressed into the wine of celebration.
Before you take that first drink, know
I'm exiled so you can carry the weight of my crown.

and I am milled by death, how will life replace me?

From a Town as Small as Muleshoe, Texas

On the path to her popularity,
she slams bottles of spirits.
The clock's metal hands
move toward last call.

Her judgment dashes down
the dark alley of no return.
She buys another round of approval;
her stool-mates heads bop yes to the beat.

She flips quarters with her tuition funds,
trades books for beers,
believes she is one of them now—
one of those girls who move in circles

that make others dizzy with envy.
Waning smoke, dwindling chatter,
mammoth silent speakers
compete for false promises of friendship.

Memories of music pound
in the back of her ears.
She sits alone at the bar,
top littered with bottles.

Her stool-mates backs
are a mockery of her innocence/delusions.
They walk away, do not wave or look back.
Their laughter is a dart,

reaches the bull's-eye of her stomach
as she watches them
spill out, become shadows.
She staggers into the faded night

with an empty wallet, heart.
The wind taps a gentle rhythm
on the drum of her cheeks.

The sun frames the nightclub's blue neon sign.
She leans on the loneliness of morning,
eyes leaking tears, betrayed by the moon.

339

Sleep carries me by the neck.
It is a prowling lioness and I am her cub.
I feel myself lifted from a plastic blue recliner
and placed upright in front of a water-streaked mirror
opening and shutting my eyes
as though this motion will make clarity flesh.

I wash my face and try to brush away
last night's fusty air from my mouth.
Why do sadness and mirth,
dreams and nightmares,
breaking and mending
have the same stale taste in the morning?

The sides of his yellow untied hazard gown
make the hospital tech look like a canary
as he flaps around the room readying her for discharge.
He holds a bedpan in his blue-gloved hands
as he chirps into his cell phone,
This is Brandon. 339 is going home.

Fully dressed, but half clutched in the lioness' mouth,
I scan the room, start packing her things.
She is Mama, the pulse of my drive
and source of my stubbornness.
To call her mother is too stiff and formal.
At this moment, I wish for the silence
camped in her throat as I take a dress off the hanger
and ask her, Mama where are your shoes?
With a voice softer than her bed sheets
she answers, I have no shoes.

With regret roaring in my stomach,
I rub my face searching for a bruise
after the lioness drops me into consciousness.
I didn't know the weight of limbs until my heart fell
in the place where Mama's legs used to be.

Randall Watson

Perishables

They shall be thanked for their softness,
Just as these fingers shall be
                                                            when they are steep with light,
Just as the feet shall be
                                                            for their tripping and sliding.

And the moon, too, shall be thanked, for its changes.

And the engines of airplanes that roar toward sleep
            on the edges of that changing light,
And sleep for the rest it gives
When we are broken by the wakefulness of thought,
                                                            the weight of addition.

Just as the horror of my mother's face shall be thanked
            when she takes her teeth out.

And the heat shall be thanked, for rising.

And I shall thank the cold for coming down,
And the zero shall be thanked
                                                            for subtracting nothing.

And someone will be there to assist me in this.

And he shall help me thank the hollow of a band shell
            for its wet face.
And he shall help me thank the voice of a man
            who clears his throat in the morning,
And the insect the amateur entomologist pries open,
And the instruments of the entomologist's fingers.

And he will be standing there and he will be my grandfather.

And there will dirt upon his overalls and his gray cap,
And he will tell me what comes, and what comes after,
And he will thank the hands of the pitcher plants

for their syrupy fingers,
And the steeple of the bittern's face when it glances upwards,
and we shall do this together.

And then one day he will not be standing.

And the morning will be there in his place
And it will make the world loud with its twitterings
And I will not be fond of its loudness,
I will want the night to close, like a dog's coat
sleek and Labrador,
And I shall want to come undone, like the laces of a shoe,
before the night is over.

But I shall not come undone, though I should like to.

And I shall seat him on a stump among the elms by the creek,
And I will make it hard to see him because the wind has risen
and the air is dusty.

So I shall imagine him there, chewing on something.

And his hands shall be busy fixing a footstool
And when he is done he will put his feet up
And there will be mud and stickers on his boots
And he shall point to the clouds that circle above us
And he shall tell me about the clash of ions in the air.

And I shall be so happy I shall thank the dirt on my fingers.

I shall thank the turnip for drawing color from the earth,
And I shall take this color into my mouth and match it
with my tongue,
And it will be like kissing my grandfather,
like putting my hand in his.

And we shall take a little plastic boat across the creek,
And we shall share a 7-UP because we are thirsty
and there will be shade on the water
And all sorts of bugs shall be flying this way and that.

And a heron also shall be walking in the mud at the creek's edge.

And we shall thank the heron's stillness when we are near
because it is the stillness of the mind,

And we shall thank its soft retreat when we approach
    because it is the mind's movement.

And I shall take the halo from its right eye
    and slip it on my finger,
And it will be like marrying my grandfather,
    like going down the aisle together.

And I shall take the halo from its left eye and save it for later.

And the right eye shall be used to rebuild
    the face of my grandfather.

And I shall return the oil to his skin, the part to his hair,
And he will be young again and we will be standing there.

And then I will give him back the halo I have saved for later.

And we will use it to look at the book we have bought to look at.

And the book will be filled with the reproductions
    of great paintings.

And there will be blood in the paintings, and a yellow light.

And an essay will tell us which of the colors have faded
And which have been cleaned and returned to brightness

Once Grief Has Entered

A pulse, you said.

Liminal. Braided.

As in that maple where the meadow lifts,
its full crown like the halo of a flare,
a mean of interbranching light
in a floating share of brown and green,
luminescent, motional.
Or that autumn outside Albany
when the trees opened
and the pond emerged
from the scratchy shadows
bright as resin.

Strange, isn't it, what sometimes hurts us.

The heron, blue and great and passing far above,
so slow and graceful it is not flight
but the sheer gentleness of air,
as it eases its way down to the willows.
How it arches its wings
and lifts for a moment,
almost weightless,
before it touches down.

William Wenthe

Hammering Stones

On the gospel channel, bodybuilders:
one rolls up a frying pan, one uncurls
a horseshoe's steel Omega; one lays hands
on a pair of Georgia license plates, rips
them in half. Leather weight-belts, talc,
sweat, glutted veins in bicep, neck;
gnashing teeth, grunts bowel-deep, pecs
that surge and stress the words
on T-shirts: GOD MADE YOU TO WIN.

It's more than just a ten-foot log
one of them cleans and jerks above his head;
nor do they believe the single-mindedness
of the man hammering stones with his forehead
is enough. That something other moves
in the knuckles of the man clobbering nails
into hickory with his fists is concrete
proof: here is Grace made tangible.

In a motel room, the thumb of a man
clicks along the remote, looking
for something to distract him from one
moment to the next. Above the neon lot,
a few stars visible, spiked into the dark;
bats lift *themselves* in jagged wreaths
around the streetlamps. All day, with one foot
and one hand, he moved 2000 pounds of Chevy
across four states. If he can lift tomorrow
his eight pound head from the damp pillow
it will be enough. The sun could do no more.

Uhte

Lately I've been waking with my infant daughter
in the hour before dawn.
We sit in the rocking chair as shades
outside the window begin their slow, emergent
separation: the darker mass of trees
looming against withdrawing, slate-toned sky
and a few stars, slightly smaller now, farther.

And I'm recalling, from my years' ago
study of Old English, a word, *uhte*:
"the hour before dawn." I've lost most
of that old tongue, but that word
has haunted me—wondering how that hour
had first called forth a need
to be distinguished by a sound.

Did that first, faint ash of light
augur grief, or gratefulness: *uht*-care
of the lamenting wife, or *uht*-song
of the monk's orison? For me,
in this fulcrum hour, it's a balance
between body's sleep-longing, and rest-
lessness of mind. But not for my daughter, full

awake, and writhing in my arms until
I have to set her down to crawl.
She keeps a running commentary as she goes,
in infant babble and chortle—but within it
a recurring sound, two syllables: distinctly
a word of her own making, whose meaning,
in her predawn of language, I can only try

to guess. Though hearing her, I'm just now
coming to realize how she's given
body to that ancient word
for an hour that most of my life
I've missed out on, but now share with her,
before it blurs into the light
of merely numbered hours.

Universes

Mountain Chickadee
A name at once so big, so small.

April Storm
Pear blossoms and snowfall, and not a metaphor.

My Daughter's Toes
Fresh from the amniotic sea, this pink anemone.

Hummingbird Nest (I)
She harvests cobwebs under the sophet.

Garden Prohibition
The Monarch is poison to the Kingbird.

Cave Swallow
What the cave does, or where the swallow lives?

Mockingbird
Pays no royalties on borrowed tunes.

Mantis
Praying or Preying, I can never remember.

Daughter at Six Months
I point to the clouds but she's looking at starlings.

Hummingbird Nest (II)
This plum-sized cup of lichen and web—how did I find it?

Stepping on an Ant
Not if it were my size.

Marilyn Westfall

On the Texas Plains

From the arid
sky,
white-blue
like a faded dress,

sparrows fall
in a flock
and whirl
above me,

their rush
of wings
a lilting
breath

that is hushed,
swept away
like seed
in the wind;

winnowed to a handful
wavering
in a gust,
they climb

to high-
tension wires
strung
between two poles,

and settle,
notes dashed
on a staff,
a solitary

bar of song.

Allyson Whipple

Final Destination

Remember that last time that you drove
together? A thousand miles from home,
an exit sheltered by a shady grove–

you thought that it might lead you back to love,
convince your heart it didn't need to roam.
Remember that last road you drove:

the effort to move on, but not to move
another's soul, or the car's old chrome.
An exit sheltered by a shady grove

did not result in cabin, cave, or cove
to protect your marriage from a tomb.
No escape, despite the road you drove.

What solace? What treasure trove
could have saved you? What lengthy tome
could fix the problem? Exit the shady grove,

drive back, following grackle and dove,
the welcome sun, clouds soft like foam.
Remember, now, the roads you drove.
Remember shelter. Your exit. The shady grove.

Mary F. Whiteside

Prairie Scenes

The white church sits forsaken, warmed by early summer sun. Rooted, beside a windbreak of aged fir trees leaning toward everlasting life. Rusted grain elevators rise toward heaven. Eight o'clock, light still high above the horizon.

prairie cathedrals
abide in realms of green and brown—
standing promises

A hundred pairs of obsidian eyes stare. Mine stare back. Nibbling grass blades, prairie dogs stand on hind legs, their gaze unshifting. I watch. A hawk circles. Barely audible barks halt the contest: eyes vanish. I linger. Here and there diminutive brown heads edge above the burrows then disappear. A waiting game.

near prairie-dog towns
expect coyotes, bison, tiny owls
pray for black-tailed ferrets

Decaying glaciers' legacy. Shallow depressions filled with snowmelt and spring rain. Some temporary, others permanent, all surrounded by grassy oceans. Spirited circles, homeplace to bulrushes and cattails, geese, ducks, and cranes. Listen to the wild, no need to strain.

crickets, frogs
a coyote's howl
muskrat ramblin' sounds

Scott Wiggerman

Love

Grackles: their very name evoking greed,
aggression, chaos. Persistent as weeds,
a black plague, they swarm in like cloying clouds
of pestilence, ill-mannered, siren-loud.
Called devil birds by some, they persecute
the neighborhood, attack my outdoor cats
as if they're prey. At dinnertime, I stand
on guard; the grackles do not wait to land
at bowls unfinished, nabbing one kibble
per lunge. But one bird brings a sudden smile,
for morsel by humble morsel, he flies
from bowl to rail to partner. Kibble flows
from beak to beak like lovers swapping spit.
The bowl cleared, together they caw, then split.

Wintry Mix

Curled like used rags
on this dishwater-gray day,
the cats have the right idea: hunker,
make yourself small, dull,
the size of a terra cotta pot.
Outside, arctic winds thrust down
and temperatures dip below freezing.
Wrapped around susceptible plants,
sheets flap like old ghosts.

A sweats and flannel,
too cold to bathe kind of day.
Soup weather, if only there were
a pot of minestrone on the stove.
The house is dark; if it had
a fireplace, a fire would be lit.

The streets are empty, no strays about.
Rain, sleet, snow—nothing yet,

but those rare white flakes might lighten
our moods; or seal us in for good.
The heater clicks on,
cycles the best it can,
and when it shuts off,
the silence is breached
by the second hand's *tick-tick*,
the *whoosh* through overhead limbs.
In the cold living room,
we scrunch like mice
in separate corners of the sofa,
getting smaller.

Formations

A quiet field of punctuation marks
becomes a murmuration: first, the lift,
despite a brutal wind, and then the shift
across the sky, from right to left in arcs
that sail in folds, a hundred wings as one,
apostrophes in sync, an aerial
display of feathers, beaks, and last, a pull
back down to earth, this sudden dance undone.

Our lungs inflate. Our breathing bellows cells
in movement: rising, falling. That's a fact.
My own heart murmurs, beats its wings the same
direction—over, over—casts its spells,
abandons them. And so . . . expand, contract:
it's how the world began, how we became.

Joe Wilkins

Letter to Liz from Houston

You never see the sun in this city.
Gray sky always between you and light,
freeways like the wings of stone birds.
I walked north today, up old Delano Street, past
shotgun shacks and scrawny trees. Broken glass
ran the gutters like water. Liquor stores were legion.
This city's cut in half by color, and both sides
make my face Yankee so it won't fit. Grandmothers
watched me. They never smiled. Yesterday,
Quinton came to class with cigarette
burns all down his neck—ripples on the dark pond
of his body. The paper says the Guadeloupe River
is still bloated in the west. From every corner
of the Third Ward you can see Houston's square shoulders,
massive shadows grieving these streets. I walked back.
I miss you. (I think of the curve of your throat,
making these words.) On the way to work each day
I see a car wreck. The traffic, the stares—bloom
of red in gray. I have over a dozen kids
who are homeless—I teach them how to add integers
and after school they stand at Chapman and Providence,
shift on their feet as I drive away. Houston's grandmothers
see right through me. I'm trying to believe love
can be shadow and stone wing, a river of glass
over its banks and rising, still rising.

Houston Sonnet

Years ago I was lost for an entire summer
in Houston. I couldn't find my way
from Delano Street, did not believe there was a door
that led out of Enrique's Pool Hall, or any path
from the cracked lip of that cup of warm beer.
I was trying to be a good junior high math teacher
but was sick in the heart, that poor burbling
organ, meaty thwack and flush of blood—it was all
too hot, and when the air-conditioner
in my classroom broke, I opened the windows,
and we all wheezed and coughed refinery smoke,
the ash of the Third Ward up in flames,
and Quinton raised his hand and asked,
Why do cities burn so easy?

Dede Wilson

Seeing Her Grandfather Weep

The craftsman says
    our heritage chestnut
        is a risk to cut
    for cupboard or desk. Often a tree
has fleshed around steel–

a horseshoe, blade or nail–
    abraded within,
        and contact with a mill-saw
    will shatter
the heart of such aged wood.

Three Green Pears in a Blue Pottery Bowl

Gentlemen,
a little bluer, please,
Liszt is whispering
to his court musicians.

Imagine a shallow bowl
with three green pears,
the clay-cold edge
blue against his mind.

My grandmother lifting
a blue enameled bowl
to catch the beat of rain.
The clarity of rainwater
she saved to wash her hair.

Rain falling on pears.

Liszt's long fingers
ringing the rim of the bowl.

Pears ripening
under the music of blue.

Miles Wilson

Keeping Track

First we establish that life is unfair.
Any familiar story will do:
A child pedaling out from between cars.
Some bored technician, bringing the tissue sample into focus.
The man, perfectly composed now, stroking himself,
deciding
it will be the first clean-looking one,
while your wife starts home from the park
on an unaccustomed route.
The sorrow of those who tried to do most things right.

They miss the point. Which is suffering.
And randomness.

I have not forgotten the bright, tiled halls
which wait for us in official buildings,
the metallic breath of circuitry seeping
out of cool rooms, the secretary
who knows what is going to happen.

This is exact damage.
Indifferent but foretold.
Worked by the word,
syllable and subsyllable.

While God's word is His whim—
writing the book as He went. Elsewhere

some are saying "The Lord's will is my delight."
I say
be good; go to heaven.
You have a score to settle.

You, Theodore Roethke

Baboon and buzzard; lizard, lamb, and shrew
Abound when I root round my furnished zoo.
I celebrate the small. When I'm outdoors
I turn to grass before the carnivores.

I keep my Yeats at home beside John Clare
And take my metaphysic from the air.
In lean times I light out for the far fields,
Wolf down what princely toad or toadstool yields.

I knew a woman once but then forgot
Myself. Our aerobatic turkey trot
Ground to a waltz that I had danced before.
I recollect myself upon the floor.

I listen for my bones' prophetic rattle,
Stay out of swimming pools around Seattle.
Contortionist, I'm hanging tough and loose,
A slick, corkscrewing gander to time's goose.

My journeys bear me through the neighborhoods
Of outermost and intimate dark woods.
I've molted till there's nothing left to shed
And learned by going where to go instead.

June Zaner

Why bees drink turtle's tears. . .

In the Amazon some bees and butterflies
drink the tears from weeping turtle's eyes
some say it's for the minerals in them, hard
to come by in the jungle, but easily found
by tracking down a sorrowful turtle who might
sit crying in the shade of an Acioa edulis tree.

Perhaps the creature was merely enjoying the
pink blossoms of the tree or chewing one of its
date-like fruits, sweet and fragrant, wonderful
treats for old turtles, lost in jungle reverie.
The bee, in its consoling act, saves its own life
and gives the turtle a chance to be useful.

The butterflies? Well, don't they make their
living by their beauty, all flutter and flick?
In their winged conceit a challenge to the blossoms?
With a taste of turtle tears simply an after-thought
like the idle dinner party guest who fingers her
wine glass before taking a sip, never guessing
at the sorrow of the grape

THE POETS

Since the late 1980s, CAROLYN ADAMS has been featured in various reading series in Houston, Austin, and other parts of Texas, such as Word Around Town, First Friday at Inprint, The Austin International Poetry Festival, FabriFaction (as part of FotoFest), as well as Gulf Coast Poets, of which she is a member. Her writing and art have been published in numerous on-line and print publications, such as *Common Ground Review*, *Caveat Lector*, and *Cenizo Journal*, among others. She has authored the poetry chapbooks, including *Beautiful Strangers* (Lily Press) and *An Ocean of Names* (Red Shoe Press), and an ekphrastic collage art chapbook, *What Do You See?* (Right Hand Pointing). Her work has been nominated for a Pushcart prize, and she was a finalist for the post of 2013 Houston Poet Laureate.

LESLIE MARIE AGUILAR originally hails from the heartland of Texas. She has served as the Poetry Editor of *Indiana Review* and received her MFA from Indiana University. She is the recipient of a National Society of Arts and Letters Chapter Career Award and the *Washington Square* Poetry Award. Her poems have appeared or are forthcoming in *Bellingham Review*, *Iron Horse Literary Review*, *Ninth Letter*, *Rattle*, *Spillway*, and *Southern Indiana Review* among others. She is the author of *Mesquite Manual* (New Delta Review, 2015) and is a Fine Arts Work Center Fellow.

LAHAB ASSEF AL-JUNDI grew up in Syria and attended the University of Texas in Austin where he graduated with a BS in Electrical Engineering. His poetry has appeared in numerous literary publications and anthologies. His latest poetry collection, No Faith At All, was published in 2014 by Pecan Grove Press. He currently lives in San Antonio, Texas.

LOU AMYX writes and builds custom pyrographic drums in the piney woods of east Texas. Her poetry appears or is forthcoming in *Prairie Gold Anthology*, *Vision/Verse Anthology*, *Southern Poetry Anthology Vol. IV*, *Puff Puff Prose and Poetry Anthology*, *200 New Mexico Poems*, *Tidal Basin Review*, *Naugatuck River Review*, *The Arena*, and at *sugarmule.com*, *qarrtsiluni.com*, and *mellusine21cent.com* as winner of the 2011 Vivienne Haigh-Wood Prize. A chapbook, *The Bracelet*, is available from Finishing Line Press.

WENDY BARKER sixth collection of poetry, *One Blackbird at a Time*, received the John Ciardi Prize for Poetry and is forthcoming from BkMk Press in 2015. Her fourth chapbook, *From the Moon, Earth Is Blue*, is also forthcoming in 2015, from Wings Press. Other books include a selection of poems with accompanying essays, *Poems' Progress* (Absey & Co., 2002), and a selection of translations, *Rabindranath Tagore: Final Poems* (co-translated with Saranindranath Tagore, Braziller, 2001). Her poems have appeared in numerous journals (including *The Southern Review*, *Poetry*, *The Gettysburg Review*, *Mid-American Review*, *Georgia Review*, and *the Southern Poetry Review*) and in many anthologies, including *The Best American Poetry 2013*. Recipient of NEA and Rockefeller fellowships among other awards, she is Poet-in-Residence and the Pearl LeWinn Endowed Professor of Creative Writing at the University of Texas at San Antonio.

CURTIS BAUER is a poet and translator; his most recent collection of poetry is *The Real Cause for Your Absence* (C&R Press, 2013); his recent translations include *Eros Is More*, by Juan Antonio González Iglesias (Alice James Books, 2014); *From Behind What Landscape*, by Luis Muñoz (forthcoming from Vaso Roto Ediciones in 2015); and Baghdad and Other Poems, a bilingual chapbook of poems by Jorge Gimeno (forthcoming from Poets@Work Press in 2015). Bauer is the publisher and editor of Q Avenue Press Chapbooks and Broadsides, Spanish Translations editor for *From the Fishouse*, and he teaches at Texas Tech University.

ALAN BIRKELBACH, a native Texan, was the 2005 Poet Laureate of Texas. His work has appeared in journals and anthologies such as *Grasslands Review*, *Borderlands*, *The Langdon Review, and Concho River Review.* He has received a Fellowship Grant from the Writer's

League of Texas, was nominated for a Wrangler and Pushcart Prizes, is a member of both the Texas Institute of Letters and The Academy of American Poets, and is the winner of the 2015 Spur Award for Best Western Poem from the Western Writers of America. He has been a featured reader at the Texas Book Festival twice. He has ten collections of poetry. His latest book, *Meridienne Verte,* is available from Purple Flag Press. He is currently serving as the editor for the Texas Poet Laureate Series published by TCU Press.

SUZETTE BISHOP teaches at Texas A&M International University in Laredo, Texas. She has published three books of poetry, *Hive-Mind* , *Horse-Minded,* and *She Took Off Her Wings and Shoes,* and a chapbook, *Cold Knife Surgery.* Her poems have appeared in many journals, including *Jellyfish Whispers, Free State Review, New Texas, Borderlands, Concho River Review, Journal of Texas Women Writers, Aries,* and in the anthologies *The Four Seasons Anthology, Imagination & Place: An Anthology, The Virago Book of Birth Poetry,* and *American Ghost: Poets on Life after Industry.* Her poems have won the *Spoon River Poetry Review* Editors' Prize Contest and Honorable Mention in the Pen 2 Paper Contest sponsored by the Coalition of Texans with Disabilities. In addition to teaching, she has given workshops for gifted children, senior citizens, writers on the US-Mexico border, at-risk youth, and for an afterschool arts program serving a rural Hispanic community.

ROBERTO BONAZZI is the author of the critically-acclaimed biography, *Man in the Mirror,* the only book on *Black Like Me* author John Howard Griffin (1920-1980). As Literary Executor for The John Howard Griffin Estate, he has edited and written introductions or afterwords for Griffin's books: *Black Like Me* (Penguin 1996, Wings 2006, and a Japanese Edition 2006); *Scattered Shadows: A Memoir of Blindness and Vision* (Orbis Books 2004); *Street of the Seven Angels* (a novel, Wings 2003); *Follow the Ecstasy,* a biography of Thomas Merton (Orbis 1993, Burns & Oates, UK ed.1993, a German ed.1994); and *Encounters With the Other* (Essays, Latitudes Press, 1997). His essays, stories and poems have appeared in approximately two hundred publications in France, Germany, the UK, Japan, Canada, Peru, Mexico and the United States, as well as in twenty-two anthologies and in publications such as *Transatlantic Review* (London), *TriQuarterly, Minnesota Review, Chelsea, New Letters, Mississippi Review, Village Voice, National Catholic Reporter, Library Journal,* and *Excelsior* (Mexico City). From 1966 until 2000, he edited and published over one hundred titles under his independent literary imprint, Latitudes Press. Born in New York City, he has lived in Mexico City and San Francisco. Presently, Bonazzi lives in San Antonio and writes a column on poetry for the *San Antonio-Express News.*

BRUCE BOND is a classical and jazz guitarist and professor of English. He earned a BA from Pomona College, an MA in English from Claremont Graduate School, an MA in music performance from the Lamont School of Music (University of Denver), and a PhD in English from the University of Denver. He is the author of a number of collections of poetry, including *The Anteroom of Paradise* (1991); *Radiography* (1997), winner of the Natalie Ornish Best Book of Poetry Award from BOA Editions; *The Throats of Narcissus* (2001); *Cinder* (2003); *Blind Rain* (2008); *Peal* (2009); *The Visible* (2012); *Sacrum* (2017); and *Blackout Starlight: New and Selected Poems 1997-2015* (2017). His poetry combines personal lyric and metaphysical inquiry as well as the influences of music and jazz musicians. Bond has received awards from the National Endowment for the Arts and the Texas Commission on the Arts. He is a professor of English at the University of North Texas in Denton, Texas, and a poetry editor of the *American Literary Review.*

ANN REISFELD BOUTTE, who lives in Houston, is a writer of poetry, essays, and feature stories. Her work has appeared in many publications including *Through a Distant Lens* travel anthology, *New Verse News,* and is forthcoming in the Mutabilis Press Houston Nature anthology. She has a Master's Degree in Journalism and has worked as a feature writer for a national wire service. She is a four-time Juried Poet in the Houston Poetry Fest.

JERRY BRADLEY, winner of the 2015 Boswell Poetry Prize, is University Professor of English at Lamar University. He is the author of 6 books including 3 poetry collections: *Simple Versions of Disaster, The Importance of Elsewhere,* and *Crownfeathers and Effigies.* A member of the Texas Institute of Letters, he has published in *New England Review, American Literary Review, Modern Poetry Studies, Poetry Magazine, Southern Humanities Review,* and other literary magazines and is poetry editor of *Concho River Review.*

MELISSA JONES BREWER was born and raised in West Texas. She holds a BA in English/Creative Writing from Texas Tech University and an MA in Playwriting from Boston University. She has had several plays produced in regional theatres across the country and recently began writing poetry. She lives near Lubbock, Texas with her husband and three mules.

As a baby, DREW BUXTON was found abandoned in a field of bluebonnets during the hottest Texas summer in history. He writes fiction, essays, and poetry, and his work has been featured in *Vice, Hobart, Fanzine,* and *The San Antonio Current* among others

CHANTEL LANGLINAIS CARLSON is an instructor of English at Texas Christian University, where she teaches Modern Drama, Modern American Poetry, creative writing, gender studies, film, and composition. She received her PhD in English with an emphasis in creative writing at the University of Louisiana at Lafayette. Her one-act play, *The Exhibit,* was published by Next Stage Press, and her poetry chapbook, *Turning 25,* was published by Nous-zot Press. Her poetry has appeared in *Truck, Ekleksographia, damselfly press, The Southwestern Review,* and *The Louisiana Review,* and her critical work has appeared in the *Interdisciplinary Humanities Journal,* and the *Louisiana English Journal.* She has also acted in five productions with The Milena Theatre Group. She recently appeared in TCU's production of *The Vagina Monologues* and directed excerpts from her own play, *The Exhibit.*

JUDITH CARSON is a displaced native of West Texas. Born in Rotan, and bred in Sweetwater, Carson has lived in Georgia for the past thirty-six years, and although she has found beauty in many places, she considers herself Texan. Carson has worked at Georgia State University since 1983 and has had poems published in the following journals: Borderlands, Texas Poetry Review, Fall/Winter 2007; Sin Fronteras/Writers Without Borders, and The LBJ Avian Life Literary Arts. In 2006, she won 1st place in the Porter Fleming Literary Competition in the poetry category. She is currently working on a chapbook which will be called *Rocked By the West Wind*—all Texas-related poems.

The work of 2013 Texas Poet Laureate ROSEMARY CATACALOS has twice been included in *The Best American Poetry,* and she has held fellowships from the National Endowment for the Arts, Stanford University's Stegner program, and the Texas Institute of Letters (TIL)/University of Texas at Austin. Her first full-length collection, *Again for the First Time,* received the 1985 TIL poetry prize and was reissued by Wings Press in 2013. Catacalos was a Visiting Scholar at Stanford University's Institute for Research on Women and Gender from 1996-2003, and is a former executive director of the San Francisco Poetry Center and San Antonio's Gemini Ink literary center.

The son of Lebanese immigrants, HAYAN CHARARA grew up in Detroit, Michigan. He earned a BA in English from Wayne State University, an MA in humanities from New York University, and a PhD in literature and creative writing from the University of Houston. He is the author of the poetry collections *The Alchemist's Diary* (2001), *The Sadness of Others* (2006), and *Something Sinister* (Carnegie Mellon, 2016). His work often explores family, loss, identity, and the experience of growing up Arab American in Detroit. Charara is the editor of the annual literary anthology *Graffiti Rag;* he also edited *Inclined to Speak: An Anthology of Contemporary Arab American Poetry* (2008). He received a National Endowment for the

Arts literature fellowship in 2009. His children's book *The Three Lucys* won the Lee & Low Books' New Voices Award Honor.

PAUL CHRISTENSEN is the author of eight collections of poetry, the latest of which is from Lamar University Press and is, in part, a send up of the mythical southwest called *The Jack of Diamonds Is a Hard Card to Play*. An earlier collection, *The Human Condition*, was a finalist for the annual poetry award given by the Texas Institute of Letters. Two other books were "Violet Crown" award winners from the Writers' League. His essays and short stories have appeared in The Madison Review, Southwest Review, Agni, Antioch Review, The Texas Observer, Parnassus, Twentieth Century Literature, Sulfur, Temblor, and many other journals. Christensen's essay, "In Praise of Bluffing," was given Antioch Review's inaugural "Distinguished Prose" award. Best American Essays included the essay in its annual "Notable Essays" list; Best American Mystery Stories listed his story, "How Frank Died" among "Other Distinguished Stories" in its annual guide. He lives in Vermont.

GEORGE DAVID CLARK is the author of *Reveille* (Arkansas, 2015), winner of the Miller Williams Prize, and his most recent poems can be found in *AGNI*, *The Believer*, *Blackbird*, *Cincinnati Review*, *FIELD*, *Measure*, *Yale Review*, *Verse Daily*, and *Poetry Daily*. The editor of *32 Poems*, he has held the Olive B. O'Connor Fellowship at Colgate University, the Lilly Postdoctoral Fellowship at Valparaiso University, and now teaches as an assistant professor at Washington and Jefferson College.

SUZANNE C. COLE, former college English instructor, enjoys being a wife, mother, and grandmother; traveling and hiking the world; and writing from a studio in the Texas Hill Country. She's been both a juried and featured poet at the Houston Poetry Fest and once won a haiku contest in Japan. Her poetry and short fiction have been nominated for Pushcart Prizes. Her book *To Our Heart's Content: Meditations for Women Turning Fifty* was published by Contemporary (now McGraw Hill). She's also published more than 500 essays, short fiction, plays, and poems in venues ranging from *Newsweek*, *Baltimore Sun*, *Houston Chronicle*, *San Antonio Express-News* to literary and commercial journals and many anthologies. Recent 2015 publications include *Sweet*, *A Quiet Courage*, *Binnacle* Ultra-Short Contest (honorable mention), A Long Story Short, *Pan's Shadow*, Iowa State University's anthology *This Guild Itself*, *VineLeaves* and *Front Porch Review*.

SARAH CORTEZ a Councilor of the Texas Institute of Letters, has numerous poems, essays, book reviews, and short stories anthologized and published in journals, such as *Rattle* and *Post Road*. Winner of the PEN Texas Literary Award in poetry, her debut poetry collection is entitled *How to Undress a Cop*. Her second book of poetry, *Cold Blue Steel*, placed finalist in the Writers' League of Texas poetry awards. An award-winning anthologist of seven volumes, she edited *Our Lost Border: Essays on Life amid the Narco-Violence*, winner of a Southwest Book Award and an International Latino Book Award. Her latest poetry anthology is *Goodbye, Mexico: Poems of Remembrance*, already short-listed for an International Latino Book Award and published by Texas Review Press. Ms. Cortez was named to the 2014-16 Texas Commission of the Arts Touring Roster and has been a recent finalist for both Texas Poet Laureate and Houston Poet Laureate.

JERRY CRAVEN serves as press director for both Lamar University Literary Press and Ink Brush Press, and he is editor-in-chief for the literary quarterly *Amarillo Bay*. He has twenty-six published books including several collections of poetry. *Foreword Magazine* named his most recent book, *Women of Thunder* (TCU Press) the best multicultural novel of 2014. www.jerrycraven.com

SHERRY CRAVEN calls both west Texas and east Texas home. She taught college English and high school Spanish and is retired. She now lives in east Texas. She has published poetry, short fiction, and creative nonfiction. Her poetry appears in English and Spanish in journals such as *AmarolloBay, Two Southwests, descant, Langdon Review, San Pedro River Review, The Texas Review, Concho River Review* as well as the anthology *Quotable Texas Women*. Her poetry appears in *Texas Poetry 2*, and her nonfiction in *Writing on the Wind*, a collection of essays about "place" in west Texas. She won the Conference of College Teachers of English 2005 poetry award. She is an editor for Ink Brush Press. Her book of poetry *Standing by the Window* was published by Virtual Artists Collection.

THOMAS CROFTS (III) comes from San Antonio where he frequented Taco Land, Taco Cabana, and the Bone Club. He played drums in the legendary SA punk band The Raging Woodies. He is now professor in the department of Literature and Language at East Tennessee State University where he teaches medieval literature and classical languages. His academic research is focused on Arthurian literature of the Middle Ages; his poems have appeared in *The Texas Observer, Tribeca Poetry Review, Born Magazine, The Upstart Crow* and *Seymour*. He lives in Johnson City, TN, with Molly, Rex, Augie, Shadow, Argos, two chickens, and a cat named Omie Wise.

NOEL CROOK is the author of *Salt Moon* (Southern Illinois University Press), winner of the 2013 Crab Orchard Review First Book Award, and the chapbook, *Canyon* (Red Dragonfly Press). Her poems have appeared in *Best New Poets 2014, New Letters, River Styx, Shenandoah* and other journals.

LOGEN CURE is a poet and teacher. She is the author of three chapbooks: *Still*, (Finishing Line Press 2015), *Letters to Petrarch* (Unicorn Press 2015), and *In Keeping* (Unicorn Press 2008). Her work also appears in *Word Riot, Radar Poetry*, IndieFeed: *Performance Poetry*, and elsewhere. She earned her MFA in Creative Writing from the University of North Carolina at Greensboro. She lives in Dallas-Fort Worth with her wife.

CAROLYN DAHL was the Grand Prize winner in the 2015 Public Poetry/MFAH ekphrastic poetry competition, Artlines2. Her essays and poems have been published in twenty-five anthologies including *Women On Poetry* (McFarland), *Goodbye, Mexico* (Texas Review Press), *Beyond Forgetting* (Kent State), and in various literary journals including *Copper Nickel, Camas, Hawaii Review, Colere, Sojourn, and Pirene's Fountain*. She is the co-author of the poetry and art book *The Painted Door Opened*, has received grants from the Texas Commission on the Arts, residencies to Hedgebrook and the Vermont Studio Center, and won a finalist award from PEN Texas in nonfiction. Also a visual artist, Dahl has shown her work in various museums and national galleries, been a guest artist on HGTV and PBS television programs, and has authored two art books: *Transforming Fabric* (F&W Books) and *Natural Impressions* (Watson-Guptill Publications). www.carolyndahlstudio.com

CHIP DAMERON is the author of a travel book and seven collections of poetry, including two published this year: *Waiting for an Etcher* (Lamar University Press) and *Drinking from the River: New and Selected Poems, 1975-2015* (Wings Press). His poems, as well as his essays on contemporary writers, have appeared in numerous journals and anthologies in the U.S. and abroad. A two-time nominee for the Pushcart Prize in poetry and a member of the Texas Institute of Letters, he lives and writes in Brownsville, Texas.

ROBIN DAVIDSON is author of two poem chapbooks, *Kneeling in the Dojo* (Finishing Line Press) and *City that Ripens on the Tree of the World* (Calypso Editions), and a full collection, *Luminous Other*, recipient of the Ashland Poetry Press's 2012 Richard Snyder Memorial Publication Prize. She is co-translator with Ewa Elzbieta Nowakowska of The New Century: Poems from the Polish of Ewa Lipska (Northwestern University Press), and is the recipient of, among other awards, a Fulbright professorship at the Jagiellonian University in Kraków, Poland and a National Endowment for the Arts translation fellowship. Davidson was named the 2015-2017 Poet Laureate for the City of Houston by Mayor Annise Parker, and was a finalist for Texas State Poet Laureate in 2017. She teaches literature and creative writing as professor of English for the University of Houston-Downtown.

WILLIAM VIRGIL DAVIS's most recent book of poetry is *Dismantlements of Silence: Poems Selected and New* (Texas Review Press, 2015). He has published five other books of poetry: *The Bones Poems*; *Landscape and Journey*, which won the New Criterion Poetry Prize and the Helen C. Smith Memorial Award for Poetry; *Winter Light*; *The Dark Hours*, which won the Calliope Press Chapbook Prize; *One Way to Reconstruct the Scene*, which won the Yale Series of Younger Poets Prize. His poems have appeared in most of the major periodicals, here and abroad, including *Poetry, The Nation, The Hudson Review, The Georgia Review, The Gettysburg Review, The New Criterion, The Sewanee Review, The Atlantic Monthly, TriQuarterly, The Harvard Review, Hopkins Review, Southwest Review*, and *The Southern Review* among many others. Davis is a past President of the Texas Institute of Letters and Professor English and Writer-in-Residence at Baylor University.

JENNIFER M. DEAN earned an MA in poetry from the University of Nebraska-Lincoln and an MFA in creative nonfiction from California State University-Fresno. Her work has most recently appeared in Crazyhorse, Midwestern Gothic, Poetry Quarterly, Off the Coast, and elsewhere. Jennifer adjuncts at Fresno City College and has three dogs whom she accidentally taught to spell 'bath' and 'walk'. She is currently working on her first essay collection.

CHRIS ELLERY is the author of three collections of poems, most recently *The Big Mosque of Mercy*, poems based on his experiences in Syria, where he was a Fulbright professor at the University of Aleppo, and on his travels throughout the Middle East. He is co-translator (with Asmahan Sallah) of *Whatever Happened to Antara*, a collection of short stories by award-winning Syrian writer Walid Ikhlassi. A member of the Texas Institute of Letters, he currently teaches poetry writing and film criticism at Angelo State University.

SYBIL PITTMAN ESTESS has lived in Houston thirty-seven years. Originally from Mississippi, she has degrees from Baylor University, University of Kentucky, and Syracuse University. She has traveled widely. She is author of five books of poetry, the latest of which is *Like That*, by Alamo Bay Press (December, 2014). Estess's other volumes include a co-written creative writing textbook and a co-edited book of critical essays on Elizabeth Bishop. Estess's recent work appears in the anthology *Down to the Dark River*, Louisiana Literature Press, and in *Texas Review*. Twice nominated for Poet Laureate of Texas (and in 2009 becoming a finalist), Estess has also been nominated for the Texas Institute of Arts and Letters three years.

Bangladeshi American poet TARFIA FAIZULLAH grew up in Midland, Texas. She earned an MFA from the Virginia Commonwealth University program in creative writing. Her first book, *Seam* (2014), won the Crab Orchard Series in Poetry First Book Award. Focused around a long sequence "Interview with a Birangona," the book explores the ethics of interviewing as well as the history of the birangona, Bangladeshi women raped by Pakistani soldiers during the Liberation War of 1971. Faizullah received a Fulbright award to travel to Bangladesh and interview the birangona. Faizullah's honors and awards include an Associated Writers Program Intro Journals Award, a Dorothy Sargent Rosenberg Prize, a *Copper Nickel* Poetry Prize, a *Ploughshares'* Cohen Award, and a Bread Loaf Writers' Conference Margaret Bridgman Scholarship in Poetry. A Kundiman fellow, she lives in Detroit where she teaches at the University of Michigan and is an editor for the Asian American Literary Review and Organic Weapon Arts Chapbook Series. Her second book is *Registers of Illuminated Villages* (Graywolf Press, 2018).

CARRIE FOUNTAIN's poems have appeared in *American Poetry Review*, *Poetry*, and *Tin House*. Her first collection, *Burn Lake*, was a winner of the 2009 National Poetry Series Award and was published by Penguin in 2010. Penguin published her second collection, *Instant Winner*, in 2014. Fountain is writer-in-residence at St. Edward's University in Austin, Texas, where she lives with her husband, the playwright Kirk Lynn, and their children.

JOHN GORMAN lives in Galveston,Texas and taught literature and creative writing at the University of Houston-Clear Lake from its founding in 1974 to his retirement and appointment as Professor Emeritus in 2014. His poems, collected in four chapbooks, have appeared in more than two dozen Texas publications with more nationally and in Canada. He directs the monthly Galveston Poets Roundtable and has long been active with the Houston Poetry Fest.

D. A. GRAY spends his time as a full-time graduate student at Texas A&M-Central Texas in the spring and fall, and as an MFA candidate at Sewanee School of Letters in the summer. Gray originally hails from Western Kentucky but, after retiring from the U.S. Army, now resides in Central Texas. Gray has published one book of poetry, *Overwatch*, Grey Sparrow Press, November 2011. His work can also be found in *Grey Sparrow Journal*, *Appalachian Heritage*, *Poetry Salzburg*, *The Good Men Project*, *O'Dark Thirty*, *94 Creations*, *Kentucky Review* and *Spark: A Creative Anthology*. His work will also be found in upcoming issues of *The Sewanee Review* and *War, Literature and the Arts*.

LAURA QUINN GUIDRY's poems have appeared in anthologies, including *In These Latitudes:Ten Contemporary Poets*, *Down to the Dark River* and *The Weight of Addition*. Her poetry has also been published in *The Texas Review*, *Concho River Review*, *descant*, *Louisiana Literature* and other journals. She was a featured poet at Poetry on the Move in San Antonio in 2012 and her work has appeared in the *San Antonio Express-News*. She grew up in New Orleans and has lived in Texas for 35 years, currently in Carmine. She coordinates literary events at the Round Top Family Library.

R. S. GWYNN was born in Leaksville (now Eden), NC, in 1948. He is a graduate of Davidson College and the University of Arkansas. For forty years he taught at Lamar University, retiring in 2016. His books include *The Drive-In* (1986), *No Word of Farewell: Selected Poems 1970-2000*, and *Dogwatch* (2014). He was the editor of the Pocket Anthology Series from Pearson/Longman, and has written criticism for many publications, including The Sewanee Review and The Hudson Review. He is currently the program director of the West Chester University Poetry Center & Conference.

ALBERT HALEY is the son of a petroleum executive and grew up in Wyoming, Colorado, and Alaska. After earning a B.A. in economics at Yale, he began his literary career by publishing stories in *The New Yorker*, *Atlantic Monthly*, and *Rolling Stone*. Two books followed, *Home Ground: Stories of Two Families* and the *Land and Exotic*, a novel. More recently he has concentrated on poetry, with poems appearing in *Rattle*, *Poems & Plays*, *The Texas Review*, *New Texas*, *Borderlands*, *Concho River Review*, and other journals. Since 1997 he has served as writer in residence at Abilene Christian University in Abilene, Texas, where he teaches creative writing and film classes.

JERRY HAMBY teaches English and humanities at Lee College in Baytown, Texas. He has published in several journals and anthologies, including *The Texas Review*, *Concho River Review*, *New Texas*, *Windhover*, *Palo Alto Review*, *Descant*, CCTE *Studies*, the *Texas Poetry Calendar*, and *Lifting the Sky: Southwestern Haiku & Haiga*. His collection *Letters Drawn in Water* was published by Pecan Grove Press. Hamby has been a Juried Poet and a Featured Poet at Houston Poetry Fest.

ALLISON ADELLE HEDGE COKE's roots are as diverse as the routes her life and poetic career have taken. She carries in her blood a mix of Huron, Metis, Cherokee, Creek, French Canadian, Portuguese, Irish, Scot, and English ancestry. She was raised in the South, with years spent in North Carolina and Texas, but also in Canada and the Great Plains. She returned to her native North Carolina, taking jobs as a fieldworker and construction worker and attending North Carolina State University. She earned her AFAW in creative writing from the Institute for American Indian Arts and an MFA from Vermont College. Her publications include the chapbook *Year of the Rat* (1996), the poetry collections *Dog Road Woman* (1997), *Off-Season City Pipe* (2005), *and Blood Run* (2006), and the memoir *Rock, Ghost, Willow, Deer*. She is associate professor of poetry and creative writing at the University of Nebraska at Kearney.

A scholar and translator as well as poet and editor, KURT HEINZELMAN is a Councilor of the Texas Institute of Letters. Poetry International cited *The Names They Found There* as a Best Book of the Year (2011). *Whatever You May Say*, his fifth book, was published in fall 2017. A judge of the International Dylan Thomas Prize for the past 11 years, Heinzelman is an Honorary Professor at Swansea University (Wales); he is also Professor of Poetry and Poetics at the University of Texas at Austin.

TONY HOAGLAND is the author of five volumes of poetry: *Application for Release from the Dream* (Fall 2015); *Unincorporated Persons in the Late Honda Dynasty*; *Sweet Ruin*, winner of the *Brittingham Prize in Poetry*; *Donkey Gospel*, winner of the James Laughlin Award of The Academy of American Poets; and *What Narcissism Means to Me*, all from Graywolf Press.

KATHERINE HOERTH's collections include *The Garden Uprooted* (Slough Press, 2012) and two chapbooks from Mouthfeel Press. Her work has been included in journals such as *Front Porch*, *Borderlands: Texas Poetry Review*, and *BorderSenses*, in addition to the *Texas Poetry Calendar*. She teaches English at the University of Texas Pan American.

MELISSA HOLM holds an MFA from The University of Mississippi. She lives in Atlanta, Georgia where she works as the Research Project Co-ordinator for The Correspondence of Samuel Beckett Project at Emory University. Her poems have appeared or will appear in *The American Poetry Journal*, *Lunch Ticket*, *The Southern Humanities Review*, and other journals. Her poetry chapbook Ab.Sin.The. is forthcoming from ELJ Publications in 2016. She also serves as an assistant poetry editor for *Fifth Wednesday Journal* and enjoys running with her husband, Matt.

CHLOE HONUM is the author of *The Tulip-Flame*, selected by Tracy K. Smith for the 2013 Cleveland State University Poetry Center First Book Prize and winner of the 2014 Best First Book of Poetry Award from the Texas Institute of Letters and the 2014 Book of the Year Award from *Foreword Review*. Honum's poems and essays have appeared in *Agni*, *The Paris Review*, *The Southern Review*, and elsewhere. She grew up in Auckland, New Zealand, and is currently a doctoral fellow at Texas Tech University.

ANN HOWELLS has served on the board of Dallas Poets Community, a 501-c-3 non-profit, since 2000. She has edited *Illya's Honey* since 1999, recently moving the journal to digital format (www.IllyasHoney.com) and conducts readings and workshops in schools, elementary through university. Her work appeared recently or is forthcoming in *San Pedro River Review*, *Licking River*, and *Fjords*, among other small press and university journals here and abroad. Her chapbooks are: *Black Crow in Flight* (Main Street Rag Publishing, 2007) and the *Rosebud Diaries* (Willet Press, 2012). Her book, *White Star, Blue Fields*, a series of Texas poems illustrated by artist Darrell Kirkley, was released in 2016 by Village Books Press. She has been interviewed on the television show, Writers Around Annapolis and read on NPR. She is a four-time Pushcart, and two-time Best of the Net, nominee.

SABA HUSAIN's poetry may be read in *Barrow Street* 2014-15. Her work has also been published in *Natural Bridge*. She was a finalist for the *New Letters* Poetry Prize, and the recipient of The Lorene Pouncey Memorial Award for best woman poet at Houston Poetry Fest in 2014. Husain was the featured reader at First Fridays Reading Series in May 2015. She studied Creative Writing at the University of Houston. Husain grew up in Karachi; she lives, works, and writes in Houston.

LINDSAY ILLICH is an Associate Professor of English at Curry College in Milton, Massachusetts, where she teaches first year and creative writing courses and coordinates the reading and writing across the curriculum program. A native Texan, she received her Ph.D. in English from Texas A&M University. Her work has appeared in publications such as *Arcadia, Cactus Heart, Coachella Review, Gulf Coast, North American Review, Occupoetry, Rio Grande Review, Salamander, Texas Coach,* and *Texas Poetry Review* and has been anthologized in *Best Poems of Kore Press 2012, Hurricane Blues: How Katrina and Rita Ravaged A Nation, Improbable Worlds: An Anthology of Texas and Louisiana Poets,* and *Tupelo Press's Thirty Days.* Illich won the Texas Review Press Breakthrough Poetry Prize for Texas, and her collection *rile & heave* was published by Texas Review Press in 2017.

GLYNN M. IRBY lives in Brazoria County, Texas, carries a BA in history from the University of Texas at Austin, including studies at University of Houston, Brazosport College, and Edinburgh University, Scotland, with subsequent graduate studies in architecture at the University of Houston. Irby is co-author of the book, *3 Savanna Blue*, has published in *Borderlands Texas Poetry Review, San Pedro River Review, Sol Magazine*, various Texas literary festival anthologies and calendars, etc., is an honorary Lifetime Member of the Gulf Coast Poets, a member of the Poetry Society of Texas, and the Galveston Poets' Roundtable. In 2006, he was selected as one of the "Bards of the Bayou" in the Houston/Galveston area. Irby is a retired Professional Member of the American Society of Interior Designers.

LUCAS JACOB's poems have appeared in dozens of journals, including *Southwest Review, Barrow Street, Unsplendid,* and *Western Humanities Review.* Anchor & Plume press released his chapbook A *Hole in the Light* in 2015. A past finalist for the *Arts & Letters* Poetry Prize and the Fish Publishing Poetry Prize, he has won the Gival Press Tri-Language Poetry Prize and the Houston Poetry Festival's Lucille Johnson Clark Memorial Award in Poetry. He is a teacher of writing at the Trinity Valley School in Fort Worth, Texas, where he also serves as Dean of Learning and Curriculum.

KATHRYN JACOBS is a poet, medievalist, and professor at Texas A & M - C, and editor of *The Road Not Taken, A Journal of Formal Poetry.* Karen Kelsay press recently published her fifth volume of poetry, *Wedged Elephant.* Her last anthology, In Transit, appeared in 2012 from David Roberts Press. Other works include 20 articles, a book (Marriage Contracts from Chaucer to the Renaissance Stage) and almost 200 poems Measure, New South, Xavier Review, Acumen (UK) and others.

MICHAEL JENNINGS was born in the French Quarter of New Orleans and grew up in East Texas and the deserts of southwestern Iran before graduating from the University of Pennsylvania and the graduate program in creative writing at Syracuse University. He is the author of nine poetry collections, most recently *Bone-Songs and Sanctuaries, New and Selected Poems* and *River Time,* winner of the 2014 Wells College Chapbook Competition. His work has appeared in *The Georgia Review, The Sewanee Review, The Southern Review, Tar River Poetry* and many other journals. He lives with his wife and dogs on one of the Finger Lakes in Upstate New York.

RICHARD E. JOINES was born in Maryville, TN, in 1967, grew up in Nashville, and now lives in Denton, TX. He earned degrees from Western Kentucky University, Wichita State

University, and the University of Florida. He has taught literature and writing at Auburn University and now at the University of North Texas. His poems and book reviews have been published by *Still: The Journal, Appalachian Heritage, Birmingham Poetry Review, Tusculum Review, The Rumpus, Contemporary Poetry Review, The Critical Flame, Southern Humanities Review*, the *Bryn Mawr Classical Review*, and the *American Literary Review*. He is the author of a chapbook of poems, Paradeisos, from Anaphora Press. He has been an NEH Fellow, a DAAD Fellow, a resident at the Blue Mountain Center, and an AWP/Intro winner.

ROGER JONES earned a BA and MA at Sam Houston State University and a PhD at Oklahoma State University. He currently teaches in the MFA program at Texas State University. He is the author of four poetry collections, including *Strata* (Texas Review Press, 1993), *Are We There Yet?* (Texas Review Press, 2008), and *Familial* (2015). His poems have appeared in various national journals over the past four decades.

FADY JOUDAH is a Palestinian-American poet and physician. He is the 2007 winner of the Yale Series of Younger Poets Competition for his collection of poems *The Earth in the Attic*. Joudah was born in Austin, Texas in 1971 to Palestinian refugee parents, and grew up in Libya and Saudi Arabia. He returned to the United States to study to become a doctor, first attending the University of Georgia in Athens, and then the Medical College of Georgia, before completing his medical training at the University of Texas. Joudah currently practices as an ER physician in Houston, Texas. He has also volunteered abroad with the humanitarian organization Doctors Without Borders. Joudah's poetry has been published in a variety of publications, including *Poetry, Iowa Review, Kenyon Review, Drunken Boat, Prairie Schooner* and *Crab Orchard Review*. In 2006, he published *The Butterfly's Burden*, a collection of recent poems by Palestinian poet Mahmoud Darwish translated from Arabic, which was a finalist for the 2008 PEN Award for Poetry in Translation. In 2012, Joudah published *Like a Straw Bird It Follows Me and Other Poems*, a collection of poems by Palestinian poet Ghassan Zaqtan translated from Arabic, which won the 2013 International Griffin Poetry Prize. His most recent book of poetry, *Alight*, was published by Copper Canyon Press in 2013.

LAURIE KOLP serves as President of Texas Gulf Coast Writers and Secretary for Beaumont Poetry Society. She authored the full-length collection *Upon the Blue Couch* (Winter Goose Publishing, 2014) and chapbook *Hello, It's Your Mother* (Finishing Line Press, 2015). Published widely, Laurie's poetry has appeared in the *2015 Poet's Market, Scissors & Spackle, Driftwood Press, Concho River Review, Pirene's Fountain*, and others. Kolp is a not-so-recent graduate of Texas A&M University and lives in Beaumont with her husband, three children, and two dogs. She also enjoys running, photography, and tutoring children with dyslexia.

NICK LANTZ is the author of four books of poetry, most recently *You, Beast*. He is the recipient of fellowships from The National Endowment for the Arts, The Bread Loaf Writers Conference, and the Wisconsin Institute for Creative Writing, and numerous awards, including the Brittingham Prize, the Felix Pollak Prize, the Bakeless Prize, the Larry Levis Reading Prize, and the Great Lakes Colleges Association New Writers Award. He has taught creative writing at the University of Wisconsin-Madison, Gettysburg College, Franklin & Marshall College, Queens University's Low-Residency MFA, and Sam Houston State University, where he is also editor of the *Texas Review*.

JIM LAVILLA-HAVELIN is the author of four books of poetry, *Counting*; the most recent, was published by Pecan Grove Press in 2010. LaVilla-Havelin is the poetry editor at the *San Antonio Express-News* and the Coordinator of National Poetry Month events in San Antonio. His work has appeared in anthologies: *Is this Forever or What?, Between Heaven and Texas, Improbable Worlds*, and *Big Land, Big Sky, Big Hair!* His work has also appeared in magazines such as *Borderlands, Blue Hole, The Enigmatist, Texas Observer*, and many Texas Poetry Calendars.

RICH LEVY is a poet and, since 1995, has served as executive director of Inprint, a literary arts nonprofit in Houston, Texas. He earned his MFA at the Iowa Writers Workshop; his poems, essays, and reviews have appeared (or will soon appear) in various publications, including *Boulevard, Callaloo, The Florida Review, The Hopkins Review, Houston Chronicle, Pool, The Texas Observer*, and others. His poetry collection *Why Me?* was published in 2009, and in 2011 Houston Press named him Houston's "best poet." He is a member of the Texas Institute of Letters and serves on the advisory board of *Gulf Coast: A Journal of Literature and Fine Art* and the editorial committee of CITE magazine. He is a jazz obsessive and has raised three children and several cats and dogs.

MICHAEL LIEBERMAN is a Houston-based poet and fiction writer and former research physician. He is the author of seven collections of poems and four novels. Texas Review Press published *Some Dark Fire, New and Selected Poems*, 1992-2016.

JANET LOWERY'poetry has been published in journals such as *Poetry East, Greensboro Review, Concho River Review*, and in anthologies such as Mutabilies Press's 2015 *Untameable City* and the 2011 *Improbable Worlds* (edited by Martha Serpas); Texas in Poetry 2 (TCU Press, 2002), the *Poetry East* collection *Who Are the Rich and Where Do They Live?* (2000), and Women's Blood (CONTINUING SAGA Press, 1981).

COREY MARKS holds a PhD in Creative Writing and Literature from the University of Houston, an MFA from the Program for Writers at Warren Wilson College, and a BA in English from Kalamazoo College. He teaches at the University of North Texas and serves, with Bruce Bond, as Poetry Editor of *American Literary Review*. *Renunciation*, a National Poetry Series selection, was published by University of Illinois Press. Poems from his recently completed second collection, *The Radio Tree*, appear in a number of journals, including *New England Review, Poetry Northwest, Ploughshares, Southwest Review, The Threepenny Review, TriQuarterly*, and *The Virginia Quarterly Review*, as well as in the anthology *Legitimate Dangers*.

JANET MCCANN is a Texas poet who has been teaching creative writing at Texas A&M since 1969. Journals publishing her work include *Kansas Quarterly, Parnassus, Nimrod, Sou'wester, Christian Century, Christianity And Literature, New York Quarterly, Tendril, Poetry Australia, McCall's*, among many others. A 1989 NEA Creative Writing Fellowship winner, she is currently Professor of English. She has also written textbooks and reference books. Her most recent poetry collection: *The Crone At The Casino*, Lamar University Press, 2013.

ANNE MCCRADY's writing appears internationally in journals, magazines and anthologies, including *Langdon Review of the Arts in Texas, Texas Review, Texas Observer* and *Her Texas*. Her book of poems, *Along Greathouse Road*, won the 2003 Edwin M. Eakin Memorial Manuscript Award, and her collection, *Under a Blameless Moon*, won the 2007 Pudding House Chapbook Prize. Her most recent collection is *Letting Myself In* from Dos Gatos Press (2013). She has edited and published three poetry chapbook anthologies: *PeaceWords, Hunger for Peace* and *Intertwined*. She is a two-time Pushcart Prize nominee and has credits as a contest judge, editor and critic. Her poems have been performed as art song and used in a variety of worship settings. A motivational speaker and peace advocate, Anne posts regularly at PoetwithaPressPass.com, SoundCloud.com/InSpiritry and InSpiritry.com. Anne lives in Tyler, TX.

WALT MCDONALD was born in 1934. A long-time resident of Texas, he served in the Air Force and is a veteran of the Vietnam War. He earned his PhD from the University of Iowa, and taught at Texas Tech University, where he is the Paul Whitfield Horn Professor Emeritus. McDonald has published more than twenty books of poetry, including *Faith is a Radical Master* (2005), *A Thousand Miles of Stars* (2004), *Climbing the Divide* (2003), and *Great Lonely Places of the Plains* (2003). Frequently concerned with landscape and place, including Texas, McDonald's work is known for its clear, narrative style and moral heft. McDonald has published over two thousand poems in journals and literary magazines. The recipient of numerous honors and awards for his work, including six awards from the Texas Institute of Letters and four Western Heritage Awards from the National Cowboy Hall of Fame, McDonald received the Bookend Award for a lifetime of contributions to Texas literature from Texas Tech University Press in 2004.

NICK MCRAE is the author of *The Name Museum* (C&R Press, 2014) and *Mountain Redemption* (Black Lawrence Press, 2013), as well as editor of *Gathered: Contemporary Quaker Poets* (Sundress Publications, 2013). His poems have appeared in *Cincinnati Review*, *Measure*, *The Southern Review*, and elsewhere. He is associate editor of *32 Poems* and is a Robert B. Toulouse Doctoral Fellow in English at the University of North Texas.

GARRETT MIDDAUGH was born in Houston, Texas, in 1953 and has lived there most of his life. He graduated from the University of Texas at Austin with an MFA in Studio Art. Garrett is a visual artist, focusing on contemporary landscape painting, and shows at two galleries, one in Houston and one in Round Top, Texas. He has numerous paintings in corporate and private collections around the state. In 2010 and 2011 he had poems published in the *Houston Poetry Anthology* in conjunction with the Houston Poetry Fest, and in 2011 he had a poem published in the *Austin Poetry Festival Anthology*. Some years ago, in his freshman year at what was then North Texas State University, he won first prize for fiction in that university's literary journal.

TERRY JUDE MILLER is from Houston, Texas. The recipient of many Poetry Society of Texas poetry awards, a Juried Poet for the 2011 and 2012 Houston Poetry Festivals, his work has been published in scores of publications including anthologies of the Austin International Poetry Festival and the Rio Grande Valley International Poetry Festival, *Live Oak Review*, *Lamplighter Review*, *Bijou Poetry Review*, *Chaffey Review*, *Foundling Review*, *Houston Literary Review*, *Boston Literary Magazine*, *the Edison Literary Review*, and the *Birmingham Arts Journal*. Miller's books of poetry, are titled: *The Day I Killed Superman*, *What If I Find Only Moonlight?* and *The Butterfly Canonical*. He is the creator of the Texas Poets Podcast.

BRYCE MILLIGAN was the founding editor of *Pax: A Journal for Peace Through Culture* (1983-1987) and *Vortex: A Critical Review* (1986-1990). He directed the Guadalupe Cultural Arts Center's literature program and was co-founder and longtime director of the San Antonio Inter-American Book Fair. He has been the publisher, editor, and book designer of Wings Press since 1995. In the last several decades, he has published hundreds of multicultural works of fiction, poetry, and history. He is also the editor of *Daughters of the Fifth Sun* (Riverhead, 1995) and *Floricanto Si* (Penguin, 1997), two anthologies of fiction and poetry by Latina writers, among other anthologies.He has published six collections of poetry, including *Alms for Oblivion* (London: Aark Arts, 2003) and *Lost and Certain of It* (Ark Aarts, 2006). His poetry and song lyrics have also appeared in numerous literary magazines. He is a recipient of the Gemini Ink Award for Literary Excellence (2011) and the St. Mary's University President's Peace Commission's "Art of Peace" Award (2012).

JONATHAN MOODY holds an MFA from the University of Pittsburgh. He's also a Cave Canem graduate fellow whose poetry has appeared in various publications such as *African American Review*, *Beloit Poetry Journal*, *Borderlands*, *Boston Review*, *The Common*, and *Harvard Review Online*. Moody, a Pushcart Prize nominee, is the author of *The Doomy Poems* (Six Gallery Press, 2012). His second collection, Olympic Butter Gold, won the 2014 Cave Canem Northwestern University Press Poetry Prize and will be released in November of 2015. He lives in Fresno, Texas, with his wife and son.

KARLA K. MORTON, the 2010 Texas Poet Laureate, is a Councilor of the Texas Institute of Letters and a graduate of Texas A&M University. Described as "one of the most adventurous voices in American poetry," she's a Betsy Colquitt Award Winner, twice an Indie National Book Award Winner, the recipient of the Writer-in-Residency E2C Grant, and authored of nine collections of poetry. She's been nominated for the Pushcart Prize, is a nominee for the National Cowgirl Hall of Fame, and established an ekphrastic collaborative touring exhibit titled: No End of Vision: Texas as Seen By Two Laureates, with Texas Poet Laureate Alan Birkelbach. Morton's work has been used by many students in their UIL Contemporary Poetry contests, and was recently featured with seven other prominent authors in *8 Voices: Contemporary Poetry of the American Southwest* (Baskerville Publishers). Her most current collection is *Constant State of Leaping* (Texas Review Press).

KATIE DARBY MULLINS teaches creative writing at the University of Evansville. In addition to being nominated for a Pushcart Prize and editing a rock 'n roll crossover edition of the metrical poetry journal *Measure*, she's been published or has work forthcoming in journals such as Hawaii *Pacific Review, Harpur Palate, Broad River Review, Big Lucks, The Evansville Review*, and she was a semifinalist in the Ropewalk Press Fiction Chapbook competition and in the Casey Shay Press poetry chapbook competition. She's also the lead writer and founder of the music blog Katie Darby Recommends.

LAURENCE MUSGROVE is professor of English at Angelo State University in San Angelo, Texas, where he teaches literature, creative writing, drawing-to-learn, and composition studies. His new collection of poetry, *Local Bird*, is from Lamar University Press. His poetry has appeared in *Concho River Review, descant, Elephant Journal, Sleet Magazine, Inside Higher Ed, Southern Indiana Review*, and *New Texas*. He blogs at theillustratedprofessor.com and cartoons at texosophy.com. He is also co-editor of *Texas Weather*, a new anthology of poetry, short fiction, and non-fiction forthcoming from Lamar University Press.

R. C. NEIGHBORS is an Oklahoma expatriate currently working on his Ph.D. at Texas A&M University, where he studies Native American literature, Southern literature, and creative writing. His work has appeared in *Tampa Review, Barely South Review, Red Earth Review, Parody*, and elsewhere.

NAOMI SHIHAB NYE first passed through Texas as a seven-year-old with her Palestinian father and Midwestern American mother. Something must really have appealed to her parents (warm winter weather? mixed cultural atmosphere?) as they chose to move to San Antonio, after living in both Ferguson, Mo. and Jerusalem, when Naomi was sixteen. She graduated from Robert E. Lee High School and Trinity University and has worked as a "wandering writer" in hundreds of schools and communities ever since. Author or editor of more than 30 books of poetry, fiction, and nonfiction for young readers and adults, she continues to love poetry most and lives with her husband, photographer Michael Nye, a block from the beloved San Antonio River in the downtown historic district.

DAVE OLIPHANT was born in Fort Worth, Texas, in 1939. He edited The Library Chronicle at the University of Texas at Austin, where he also taught as a senior lecturer in Rhetoric and Writing, before retiring in 2006. Among his books are *The Pilgrimage: Selected Poems*, 1962-2012 (Lamar University Press, 2013), *KD: a Jazz Biography* (Wings Press, 2012), *The Cowtown Circle* (Alamo Bay Press, 2014), *Harbingers of Books to Come: A Texan's Literary Life* (Wings Press, 2009), his translation of Nicanor Parra's *Discursos de sobremesa* (as *After-Dinner Declarations*, Host Publications, 2009, winner of the book translation award from the Texas Institute of Letters for 2011), and his collection of essays and book reviews, *Generations of Texas Poets* (Wings Press, 2015). An earlier work, *Maria's Poems* (Prickly Pear Press, 1987), won an Austin Book Award. He and his Chilean wife Maria live in Cedar Park.

CARL "PAPA" PALMER of Old Mill Road in Ridgeway, Virginia, now lives in University Place, Washington. After twenty years of military assignments that include El Paso, Texas, and Schweinfurt, Germany, Palmer has been writing poetry for some time, having garnered nominations for many prizes, including the Pushcart.

DAVE PARSONS, 2011 Texas State Poet Laureate, is a recipient of an NEH Dante Fellowship to SUNY Geneseo, the French-American Legation Poetry Prize, and the Baskerville Publisher's Prize. He was inducted into The Texas Institute of Letters in 2009. Parsons has published seven poetry collections. His latest are *Reaching For Longer Water* and *Far Out Poems of the 60's*, co-edited with Wendy Barker. He is founder and co-director of the Montgomery County Literary Arts Council Writers In Performance Series and has taught Creative Writing at Lone Star College since 1992. Parsons has four grown children and lives with wife Nancy, an award winning Artist and Graphic Designer in Conroe, Texas. www.daveparsonspoetry.com

BRADY PETERSON lives near Belton, Texas where for much of the past twenty-nine years he worked building homes and teaching rhetoric. His poems have appeared in *New Texas, Windhover, Nerve Cowboy, Boston Literary Magazine, The Journal of Military Experience, all roads will lead you home, Blue Hole*, and *San Antonio Express-News*. He is the author of *Glued to the Earth, Between Stations*, and *Dust*.

JOHN POCH was the Colgate University Creative Writing Fellow from 2000-2001 and was the 2007 Thornton Writer-in-Residence at Lynchburg College. His most recent book, *Dolls*, was released in September 2009 with Orchises Press. Two *Men Fighting with a Knife* (Story Line Press 2008) won the Donald Justice Award. His first book, *Poems*, was published in January 2004 by Orchises Press and was a finalist for the PEN/Osterweil prize. *The Essential Hockey Haiku* (a poetry/fiction collaboration with Chad Davidson) was published by St. Martin's Press in Fall 2006. A limited edition letterpress/art book,*Ghost Towns of the Enchanted Circle* was published by Flying Horse Editions in 2007. Poch was a recipient of the "Discovery"/The Nation Prize in 1998.

MICHAEL G. RATHER, JR.'s work has appeared in *The Swamp Lilly Review, The Greensboro Review, The Rio Grande Review, Printer Devils' Review, Flyways*, and many other print and online journals. He has performed his poetry through the United States. Currently, he teaches composition and literature at Lamar State College-Orange and is pursuing a PhD in Creative Writing at the University of Louisiana in Lafayette.

CLEATUS RATTAN, 2004 Texas State Poet Laureate, is a former Marine, a former working and rodeo cowboy, who recently retired as Mayborn professor of English at the University of Mary Hardin-Baylor. Author of numerous collections of poetry, Rattan lives in Cisco, Texas, with his wife, Connie. His most recent collection is *A Popular Play: New & Selected Poems* (Texas Review Press, 2015).

MACKENZIE REGIER critical and creative work has been published in *Thin Air Magazine* and *The Journal*.

Besides publishing in journals such as *Kalliope, Concho River Review, Sow's Ear*, and *Southwest Review, Mochila Review, Langdon Review*, as well as anthologies such as PST's *Book of the Year, Southern Poetry Review*, and *Her Texas*, CHARLOTTE RENK has published three books of poetry, *These Holy Hungers: Secret Yearnings from an Empty Cup* (Eakin Press Manuscript Award), *Solidago, an Altar to Weeds* (Poetry in the Arts), and *The Tenderest Petal Hears*, (co-winner, 2014 Blue Horse Press Award, sponsored by San Pedro River Review). She has won Southwest's national Story Teller Award, Teacher of the Year, and Innovator of the Year Award as well as numerous other awards for and publications of poetry and fiction. Currently, she lectures and conducts writing workshops, and continues to love living in her small cabin nestled in East Texas where she walks wooded trails, jotting notes for poetry and short stories.

The poems, reviews, and essays of CAROL COFFEE REPOSA have appeared or are forthcoming in *The Atlanta Review, Southwestern American Literature, The Evansville Review, The Coal City Review, The Texas Observer, The Valparaiso Review*, and other journals and anthologies. Author of four books of poetry—*At the Border: Winter Lights, The Green Room, Facts of Life*, and *Underground Musicians*—she has received three Pushcart Prize nominations, along with three Fulbright-Hays Fellowships for study in Russia, Peru, Ecuador and Mexico and has been named the Texas Poet Laureate for 2018. A professor emerita of English at San Antonio College, she serves as poetry editor of *Voices de la Luna* and is one of the winners of the San Antonio Public Library Arts and Letters Award for 2015.

SALLY RIDGWAY is a longtime Houstonian whose poetry has been published in Texas anthologies including *Big Land, Big Sky, Big Hair, The Weight of Addition* and *Improbable Worlds* and in literary journals including *Gulf Coast* and *The Texas Review* and the newspaper *The Texas Observer*. She has taught creative writing through Writers in the Schools and The C. G. Jung Center and English at high schools in Galveston and Houston and at Houston Community College. She has an MFA in Writing from Vermont College.

JOSÉ ANTONIO RODRÍGUEZ's latest book is the memoir *House Built on Ashes*. His work has appeared in *The New Yorker, Poetry, The New Republic*, and elsewhere.

PAUL RUFFIN was director of Texas Review Press and editor of *Texas Review* for over three decades. His fiction, poetry, and essays were published in hundreds of journals, and he freely and gladly helped many Texas writers (and writers beyond the state) begin their careers. He published numerous collections of poetry, essays, and fiction. Without Ruffin's influence, Southern letters would not be nearly as vibrant as they are today. His favorite anecdote involved Eudora Welty, who said to him, "You look like a Florentine painting!"

MO H SAIDI, physician and writer, was born in Iran, moved to the United States, and became a U.S. citizen in 1975. Saidi has published numerous scientific papers and a medical textbook, and in 2007 earned an MA in English and American Literature and Language from Harvard University. Saidi has published three collections of poetry, a collection of short fiction, *The Garden of Milk and Wine*, and recently a novel, *The Marchers: A Novel*. Saidi's poems have won state and national awards and have been published in many Texas-based and national anthologies, as well as regional and national literary journals.

JAN SEALE the 2012 Texas Poet Laureate, lives seven miles from the Texas-Mexico border in the Lower Rio Grande Valley. She has taught at three universities. Her poems are collected in nine volumes: *Bonds, Sharing the House, Believing is Seeing, The Yin of It, Valley Ark, The Wonder Is, Nape, Jan Seale: New and Selected Poems*, and *The Parkinson Poems*. Seale's prose writings include two books of short fiction, *Airlift* and *Appearances*, as well as a textbook on writing family stories and a book of essays. Her plays have received performances in Texas and Massachusetts. Seale's latest book, a memoir of family creativity, is titled *Nature Nurture Neither*.

MARTHA SERPAS has published three poetry collections, *The Diener* (LSU, 2015), *The Dirty Side of the Storm* (Norton, 2007) and *Côte Blanche* (New Issues, 2002). In addition to degrees creative writing from Louisiana State, New York University, and the University of Houston, she holds a master of divinity from Yale Divinity School. Her work has appeared in *The New Yorker, The Nation*, the *New York Times Book Review, Southwest Review, Image*, and in anthologies such as *The Art of the Sonnet* and the Library of America's anthology *American Religious Poems*. Active in efforts to restore lost wetlands, she co-produced *Veins in the Gulf*, a documentary about coastal erosion. She is currently on the faculty of the Creative Writing Program at the University of Houston. She serves biannually at Tampa General Hospital as a hospital trauma chaplain.

CHRISTOPHER STEPHEN SODEN's collection *Closer* was released by Rebel Satori Press in 2011. In 2014, his play, *Water*, was produced at TeCo Theatre's LGBT Play Festival. Soden's honors include: Yaddo Fellowship and a Full Fellowship to Lambda's Retreat for Emerging LGBT Voices. In 2007, Queer Anarchy received Dallas Voice's award for Best Stage Performance. Soden received his MFA from Vermont College in January of 2005. He has been published in *Glitterwolf*, *The Gay & Lesbian Review*, *A Face to meet the Faces*, *Ganymede Poets*, *Assaracus*, *The Texas Observer*, *Sentence*, and *Borderlands*.

MELISSA STUDDARD Melissa Studdard is host of VIDA *Voices & Views*, an editor for *American Microreviews and Interviews*, and a judge for the monthly *Goodreads ¡Poetry! Group* contest. She is also the author of the novel, *Six Weeks to Yehidah*, and a collection of interviews, *The Tiferet Talk Interviews*. Her awards include the Forward National Literature Award and the International Book Award, among others. Her poetry, fiction, essays, reviews and articles have appeared in a wide range of publications, including *Poets & Writers*, *Tupelo Quarterly*, *Psychology Today*, *Pleiades*, and the Academy of American Poets' *Poem-A-Day*.

GARY D. SWAIM, educated in the public schools in California, received his AB in English from the University of California at Riverside and his PhD in Comparative Literature and Philosophy from the University of Redlands and Claremont Graduate University in California. A faculty member in the Master of Liberal Studies Program at S.M.U., Swaim serves as Faculty Advisor for the Creative Writing concentration and Executive Editor for Pony Express(ions). A broadly published poet (including two chapbooks), produced playwright, and published writer of short fiction, Swaim is additionally honored as Minnie Stevens Piper Professor of Excellence for the State of Texas and the 2011 Texas Senior Poet Laureate.

CARMEN TAFOLLAis the author of more than twenty-five books of poetry, short stories, children's work, and nonfiction. The first city Poet Laureate of San Antonio from 2012 to 2014 and state Poet Laureate of Texas in 2015, she is considered one of the madrinas of Chicana literature and is noted as a master of code-switching and trans languaging. The recipient of numerous Awards including the Americas award, two Tomas Rivera book awards, the Charlotte Zolotow, and the Art of Peace award, she lives in San Antonio, where her family has resided through more than six flags. She is a professor of bicultural bilingual studies at the University of Texas San Antonio.

LARRY D. THOMAS, a member of the Texas Institute of Letters, served as the 2008 Texas Poet Laureate. He has published several award-winning collections of poetry, and in numerous prestigious national journals including the *Arkansas Review*, *Callaloo*, *Chattahoochee Review*, *Green Hills Literary Lantern*, *Louisiana Literature*, *Midwest Quarterly*, *San Pedro River Review*, *Southwest Review*, *Southwestern American Literature*, *Texas Review*, *Town Creek Poetry*, and *Valparaiso Poetry Review*. *As If Light Actually Matters: New & Selected Poems*, the most comprehensive and definitive collection of his poetry to date, was issued by Texas Review Press (Member, Texas A&M University Press Consortium) in Spring 2015. Among his many honors/awards are two *Texas Review* Poetry Prizes, two Western Heritage Awards (Western Heritage Museum, Oklahoma City, Oklahoma), the Violet Crown Book Award (Writers' League of Texas), nomination for the 2007 Poets' Prize (Nicholas Roerich Museum), and six Pushcart Prize nominations.

SIDNEY THOMPSON's poems, from a series titled *You/Wee*, address his daughter, Emerson, throughout the stages of her early development, from embryo to three-year-old. They have previously appeared in *A capella Zoo*, *Avatar Review*, *Burningword Literary Journal*, *The Fat City Review*, *The Fertile Source*, *IthacaLit*, *Literary Juice*, *Literary Mama*, and *RHINO Poetry* (with one reproduced in audio format on Big Horn Blog). He is also the author of the short story collection *Sideshow*, which *ForeWord Magazine* awarded the Silver Award for Best Collection of 2006. His stories have appeared in a variety of anthologies of Southern literature, and in such journals as *The Carolina Quarterly* and *The Southern Review*. He holds an M.F.A. in creative writing from the University of Arkansas and a PhD in American literature from the University of North Texas. He lives in Fort Worth, where he teaches writing at Texas Christian University.

JONATHAN TRAVELSTEAD served in the Air Force National Guard for six years as a firefighter and currently works as a full-time firefighter for the city of Murphysboro. Having finished his MFA at Southern Illinois University of Carbondale, he now works on an old dirt-bike he hopes will one day get him to the salt flats of Bolivia. He has published work in *The Iowa Review*, on *Poetry Daily*, and the *Crab Orchard Review*, among others. His first collection, *How We Bury Our Dead*, was published in 2015 by Cobalt Press.

NATALIA TREVIÑO's first collection of poetry, *Lavando La Dirty Laundry*, was published by Mongrel Empire Press. My poems have won the Alfredo Moral de Cisneros Award, the Wendy Barker Creative Writing Award, the Dorothy Sargent Rosenberg Poetry Prize, and the San Antonio Artist Foundation Literary Prize. They have appeared in several literary journals including *Bordersenses, Borderlands: Texas Poetry Review, Sugar House Review, Sliver of Stone Magazine, burntdistrict, The Houston Literary Review*, and *Voices de la Luna*. My non-fiction essays appear in *Shifting Balance Sheets: Women's Stories of Naturalized Citizens* and *Complex Allegiances: Constellations of Immigration*.

JOSEPH R. TROMBATORE is an artist and poet whose work has appeared in: *Travois: An Anthology of Texas Poetry, Right Hand Pointing* (online), *Journal of the American Studies Association of Texas*, and elsewhere. His poetry collection, Screaming at Adam, was awarded the Wings Press Chapbook Prize in 2007, and one of his poems received the 2011 Larry D. Thomas Poetry Prize (REAL: Regarding Arts & Letters). Other honors include two Pushcart Prize nominations and a Best of the Net Anthology nomination. Former Poetry Editor of: The Houston Literary Review (online) and Founder/Publisher of the defunct online journal, *Radiant Turnstile*, he now resides in San Antonio.

A German born in South Africa, RONJA VIETH holds a Ph.D. in American Gothic Literature from Texas Tech University, loves Texas, and has been writing poetry ever since she could hold a pen. Besides her extensive academic presentations and publications she read poetry and nonfiction at conferences in Wales (UK) and the USA and has published in national as well as international journals, such as the *The Lindenwood Review, ROAR Magazine, Linden Avenue Literary Journal, Brooklyn Review, Bohemia Journal, Sugar Mule* - Women Writing Nature, *Brooklyn Review*, The *Taj Mahal Review* (India), *The Southwestern Review*, and *Life is but a Verse – well-rhymed and bold* (Germany). During her residence in Lubbock, Texas, she also was manager of and participant in the city's poetry group Jak's Line.

CELINA VILLAGARCIA's roots are in the Rio Grande Valley, Texas. She earned her B.A. in Sociology at Metropolitan State University of Denver. She also received a Masters of Arts in Theology at Oblate School of Theology in 2012. She has lived in San Antonio, Texas for the past fifteen years where she and her husband, Paul, find great pleasure in raising their four children, ages 13 to 21. Two of her poems "Instead of Barbie" and "Prayer for Tía Susie" were finalists in the 2012 Provincetown OuterMost Poetry Contest, judged by Marge Piercy. Her first book of poetry *Pulp* (Mouthfeel Press) was published in 2013. Her work has appeared in *Texas Poetry Calendar, San Antonio Express-News*, and various journals including *Forge Journal, Acentos Review*, and *The Café Review*. She currently speaks about her journey in the borderlands and conducts writing workshops.

LORETTA DIANE WALKER won the Phyllis Wheatley Book Award for *In this House* (Bluelight Press). She was named "Statesman of the Arts" by the Heritage Council of Odessa. She was recently the featured poet in *Red River Review* (February 2017). Her work has appeared in various literary journals and anthologies. She has published four collections of poetry. Her most recent collection is *Desert Light* (Lamar UP).

RANDALL WATSON's *The Sleep Accusations* received the Blue Lynx Poetry Prize at Eastern Washington University, and is currently available through Carnegie Mellon University Press. His first book, *Las Delaciones del Sueno*, translated by Antonio Saborit with an Introduction by Adam Zagajewski, was published in a bi-lingual edition by the Universidad Veracruzana in Xalapa, Mexico. His novella, Petals, (under the heteronym Ellis Reece) received the *Quarterly West* Prize in the novella. He is also the editor of *The Weight of Addition* (Mutabilis Press), an anthology of Texas poetry. His poems have appeared in various journals and anthologies, including *Chelsea, Shenandoah, The Georgia Review, Litéral, Criterion, Portland Review, Goodbye Mexico,* and *Far Out: Poems of the 60's.*

WILLIAM WENTHE's fourth book of poems is *God's Foolishness*, published by LSU Press in 2016; his other books are *Words Before Dawn* (LSU, 2012), Not Till We Are Lost (LSU, 2004) and Birds of Hoboken (Orchises Press, 1995, reprint 2003). He has received poetry fellowships from the National Endowment for the Arts and the Texas Commission on the Arts, and two Pushcart Prizes. His poems have appeared widely in journals and anthologies, and his critical essays on the craft of poetry have appeared in *The Yale Review, Kenyon Review,* and *American Poetry Review*. Born and raised in New Jersey, he received a PhD in English from the University of Virginia, and teaches creative writing and modern poetry at Texas Tech University.

MARILYN WESTFALL has published poetry, fiction, essays, and interviews over many years, including her April 2015 interviews with three Texas poets laureate in *Lone Star Literary Life*. Most recently, her poetry has appeared in *Pilgrimage Magazine, Right Hand Pointing, Gravel Magazine, Southwestern American Literature, Illya's Honey, Red River Review,* and *Concho River Review*. New poems are forthcoming in *Mezzo Cammin*. She holds a PhD in Literature and Creative Writing from Texas Tech University.

ALLYSON WHIPPLE has an MA in English and a black belt in kung fu. She is the author of the chapbook *We're Smaller Than We Think We Are* (Finishing Line Press). Her collaborative projects include the interactive fiction *Choice: Texas*, as well as co-editing the 2016 and 2017 editions of the *Texas Poetry Calendar*. Allyson is currently enrolled in the University of Texas at El Paso Online MFA program. She teaches at Austin Community College.

MARY F. WHITESIDE grew up in the Ohio foothills of the Appalachians, but now calls the Texas prairie home. Never without a notebook in her backpack, she enjoys writing about rural areas, especially in the southern and western United States. Short fiction and haibun, often with an element of history, captivate her imagination. Her writing has appeared in *Lifting the Sky: Southwest Haiga and Haiku, Contemporary Haibun Online, Haibun Today, 200 New Mexico Poems, Forces Literary Journal,* and *Star 82 Review*. Whiteside is currently working on the life of Lucy Audubon, John James Audubon's wife. A rare bird, Lucy Audubon helped John Audubon define his dream of publishing Birds of America and supported herself and their two sons while John spent years hunting and drawing. Lucy will tell her story through diaries, notes, letters, poems, and found objects.

SCOTT WIGGERMAN is the author of three books of poetry—*Leaf and Beak: Sonnets; Presence;* and *Vegetables and Other Relationships*. He is co-editor of several Dos Gatos Press publications, including *Wingbeats: Exercises and Practice in Poetry, Wingbeats II,* and *Lifting the Sky: Southwestern Haiku and Haiga*. His poems have appeared in the anthologies *This Assignment Is So Gay; The* Great Gatsby *Anthology; Pushing the Envelope: Epistolary Poems; The Crafty Poet; Forgetting Home: Poems about Alzheimer's;* and *The Queer South*. Other recent poems have appeared in *Red Earth Review, Frogpond, Borderlands: Texas Poetry Review, The Road*

Not Taken, and *The Zen Space*. After thirty-five years in Texas, Wiggerman and his husband, the writer David Meischen, moved to New Mexico in 2015, along with Dos Gatos Press. Currently editing an anthology of Southwest persona poems, Wiggerman and Meischen continue to publish the *Texas Poetry Calendar*, now beginning its nineteenth year.

JOE WILKINS is the author of a memoir, *The Mountain and the Fathers*, winner of a 2014 GLCA New Writers Award—an honor that has previously recognized early work by the likes of Richard Ford, Louise Erdrich, and Alice Munro—and two collections of poetry, *Notes from the Journey Westward* and *Killing the Murnion Dogs*. A Pushcart Prize winner and National Magazine Award finalist, Wilkins has published essays, poems, and stories in *The Georgia Review*, *The Southern Review*, *The Sun*, *Orion*, *Ecotone*, and *Slate*. Wilkins lives with his wife, son, and daughter in the Willamette Valley of Oregon, where he teaches writing at Linfield College.

DEDE WILSON's latest collection, *Near Waking*, was published by Finishing Line Press. Her previous collections include *Glass*, finalist for the Persephone Press Award; *Sea of Small Fears*, winner of the Main Street Rag Chapbook Competition; *One Nightstand*, light verse in forms with a primer to poetic forms, and *Eliza: The New Orleans Years*. Published by Main Street Rag, *Eliza: The New Orleans Years* was a finalist for the Perugia Press Award and the Pearl Poetry Prize. Four poems from Eliza appeared in *Nimrod* as finalists for the Pablo Neruda Award, and one was nominated for a Pushcart by the *New Orleans Review*. *Eliza* has been performed as a one-woman show in Jackson, MS, and Charlotte, NC. Wilson's poems have been published in *Spoon River Poetry Review*, *Carolina Quarterly*, *South Carolina Review*, *Flyway*, *Poem*, *The Lyric*, *Tar River Poetry*, *Southern Poetry Review*, *Asheville Poetry Review*, *Cream City Review* and many other journals. She lived in Dallas from 1960 to 1967, where she was travel editor of *The Dallas Times Herald*. A resident of Charlotte, NC, since 1967, her work also appeared in the North Carolina volume of *The Southern Poetry Anthology*.

MILES WILSON's poetry has appeared widely in journals, including *The Georgia Review*, *The North American Review*, *Poetry Northwest*, *The Sewanee Review*, *Massachusetts Review*, *Southern Poetry Review*, and *Poetry*. His collection of poems, *Harm*, published in 2003 by the University of Nevada Press, won two book awards and was shortlisted for two others. *Line of Fall* (University of Iowa Press, 1989) won the John Simmons Short Fiction Award. Wilson's novel *Fire Season* won the Stephen F. Austin State University Press Fiction Prize and was published in 2014. Wilson has held fellowships from the Writers' League of Texas, the Christopher Isherwood Foundation, and the National Endowment for the Arts and is a member of the Texas Institute of Letters.

Born in Oklahoma City in 1937, JUNE ZANER is married to Richard M. Zaner and has two children, Melora and Andrew. She has been an active visual artist since 1957. Her work has been in various media: steel-welding, stone-carving, soft sculpture, pen and ink, water color, oil, soft-wares, wearable art, and theater pieces. After a long, successful career in them, she returned to writing, primarily poetry. After her husband retired, she works from her current home: 18213 Barbuda Lane in Nassau Bay, Houston, TX.

Acknowledgements

All poem copyrights immediately revert back to respective authors, and Texas Review Press has permission from the authors to reprint poems included herein.

CPSIA information can be obtained
at www.ICGtesting.com
Printed in the USA
FFOW02n2214100418
46222565-47551FF

9 781680 030631